School Desegregation

SCHOOL DESEGREGATION OUTCOMES FOR CHILDREN

Nancy H. St. John
University of Massachusetts, Boston

With a Foreword by
NATHAN GLAZER

A WILEY-INTERSCIENCE PUBLICATION

JOHN WILEY & SONS, New York • London • Sydney • Toronto

Copyright © 1975, by John Wiley & Sons, Inc.

All rights reserved. Published simultaneously in Canada.

No part of this book may be reproduced by any means, nor transmitted, nor translated into a machine language without the written permission of the publisher.

Library of Congress Cataloging in Publication Data

St. John, Nancy Hoyt.
    School desegregation.

    "A Wiley-Interscience publication."
    Bibliography: p.
    1. School integration—United States. I. Title.

LA210.S28   370.19'342   74-18492
ISBN 0-471-82633-2

Printed in the United States of America
10 9 8 7 6 5 4 3 2 1

Foreword

This introduction is being written during the first weeks of Boston school desegregation while the newspapers are daily filled with stories of how desegregation is progressing — or not — and the local television stations regularly show pictures of columns of buses protected by masses of policemen making their way from one area of the city to another. There are varying interpretations to these harrowing scenes: that 21 years after the Supreme Court decision declaring segregation unconstitutional the nation is still racist; or that the North is even more racist than the South; or, we may conclude, that something has gone terribly wrong with our effort as a nation to right a monstrous wrong.

I believe any reader of Dr. St. John's sober and elegant book will come up with the last interpretation. This book is to my mind the single most important contribution social scientists have made to the agonizing problem of school integration. It is not yet another study of school integration in this or that place, under these or those circumstances. It is not another reanalysis of the great and valuable and yet somewhat ambiguous mass of data of the 1966 Coleman Report. Dr. St. John has herself made significant contributions to the research on desegregation;

but here she reviews *all* the research available, about 120 studies, and asks a question that has recently been sadly ignored: what does it do for, and to, children? She has put aside questions of constitutional interpretation or of political significance, and has asked the question that most of us consider the most important one and that in fact provided part of the reasoning for the original constitutional decision on desegregation.

And what she demonstrates, overwhelmingly, is how simple and simple-minded our understanding of that question has been — and in "our" I include the social scientists who have been an important force in the movement for legal desegregation, the lawyers who used their arguments, the judges who imposed their interpretations. There was no reason to believe that desegregation alone — the achieving of some statistical mix of children of different races — would raise the educational achievement of black children, enhance their self-image, or improve race relations. Indeed, the evidence to date demonstrates that to expect a clear result from *one* change in a situation, without considering everything else that is crucially important in children's lives, was naive. Was the integration "natural" — a result of neighborhood mixing? voluntary — a result of choice? forced — a result of state or judicial compulsion? How was it seen by the different groups involved? How was it carried out? When was it carried out? What did it mean symbolically — did it mean the expansion of opportunity and freedom or the restriction of choice by arbitrary authority?

How all this could have been ignored, to play no role in the development of integration programs, is hard to understand: in the end, a line of constitutional interpretation was developed and imposed that permitted hardly any variation, no adaptation to circumstance, no role for educators, and no concern for the education of children.

Whether or not one sees the development of integration policy in this country in this way or not — and I have expressed my own view, not Dr. St. John's — it will be hard for any reader of this book to disagree that if one does have concern for "outcomes for children," integration policies must be much more subtle, varied, modulated, based on concrete realities and continuing research than they have been to date.

I hope that this book will speedily find its way into the hands of judges and lawyers and schoolmen now struggling with problems of desegregation and integration; it cannot help but make them more modest, more knowing, and more humane.

NATHAN GLAZER

Harvard University
Cambridge, Massachusetts
October 1974

Preface

My aim in undertaking this book was to contribute one approach to the rounded evaluation of desegregation to date that I believe citizens and educators need. To this end I try to make available to the lay reader the findings of over 100 studies of the effects of desegregation on children. I weigh this evidence in terms of the methods by which it was gathered, consider its meaning, and suggest the policy implications as I see them.

Objectivity is especially important and especially difficult to achieve when the topic is as controversial and emotionally charged as the one before us. We cannot ignore the possibility that, among the studies about to be reviewed, some have been affected by political considerations or by the unconscious bias of the investigator; see Pettigrew (1969) and Wolf (1972) on the dangers of "managed research" and exaggerated reporting. Nor is this reviewer immune to unconscious bias. A brief account of how this study developed may put the reader in a stronger position to judge for himself.

My education in segregation and desegregation began in 1948 when my family moved to Fisk University, a leading black institution in Nashville, Tennessee. For the next seven years we lived on the campus. My husband was at first assistant to

President Charles Johnson, later academic dean; I was on the teaching faculty and directed the International Student Center. The first fall I started an interracial nursery school in our home; this was taken over by the university the next year, but some of our own children continued in the school for 4 years. The older children participated in many interracial activities on campus (dancing, theater, Little League, Sunday school), but for their formal schooling they were ferried across town, together with children of other white faculty, to Peabody College Demonstration School, there being no biracial grade school in Nashville in those years. Our children learned a sad lesson: they had to keep their two lives separate and not tell of campus friends and doings while at school or talk about school life while with campus friends.

While at Fisk we became vividly aware of the social costs of legal school segregation. When we moved North in 1954 I worked in the Fair Housing movement for several years and saw how inevitably northern residential segregation leads to de facto school segregation. An interview study with Rhode Island high school graduates in 1958 reinforced my conviction as to the importance of integrated schooling for the entry of black youth into the mainstream of American life. (St. John, 1958)

My commitment to ingegration led me to undertake my first study of the effects of segregation in New Haven, Connecticut, in 1962. I was sure that the hypothesized positive relation between the percentage white of a child's elementary school and his later performance in high school would receive clear support and would be useful evidence in court cases. Unfortunately that hypothesis was not confirmed. I interpreted the lack of significant difference as due to various methodological limitations (small sample, low degree of segregation in the city, etc.). (St. John, 1962)

For my next study of the effect of school racial composition I chose Pittsburgh, Pennsylvania, a city where the number of segregated and desegregated elementary schools and available sample of black students were much larger. In this study psychological as well as academic outcomes were measured. But again the results were disappointing. No difference was found in the reading scores and self attitudes of desegregated and segregated youth, aspirations were significantly higher in segregated schools, and only arithmetic showed the expected boost from early desegregation. (St. John, 1969)

I then reasoned that the family and classroom situation must be powerful intervening variables which prevented school racial composition from showing the expected relation to children's achievement and attitudes. Therefore in Boston a study was designed with week-long observations in each elementary classroom in the sample, along with interviews with teachers, principals, and mothers. Again the findings did not strongly support the basic hypothesis that desegregation confers clear benefits. However, as I had guessed, various individual and situational variables apparently conditioned its impact on children. (St. John, 1974)

During the years spent gathering and analyzing empirical data on this topic, I also followed the results of all other such studies found in published and unpublished sources. As the reviews in the following chapters indicate, the differences between segregated and desegregated children on any outcomes that have been tested are seldom large. All studies to date, my own included, have their methodological limitations, the most important being short time span and inadequate control of family background. Nevertheless, I have come slowly to the conclusion that the overall inconclusiveness of the findings is due not so much to these limitations as to the fallacious assumption that desegregation is a unitary phenomenon, that racial balance is *the* important variable, and that how it is implemented is of secondary importance.

The theme that will be developed in this book is that school desegregation is a many-sided phenomenon, whose effects may be simultaneously beneficial to children in some respects and detrimental in other respects. Whether the potential benefit out-weighs the potential harm depends not only on characteristics of individual pupils involved but above all on how well schools adapt to meet the challenge of a biracial population. For too long courts, legislatures, schoolmen, and social scientists have been obsessed with questions of quantity rather than quality, with mathematical ratios, quotas, and balance, rather than with the educational process itself. The real task — to translate desegregation into integration — still remains.

NANCY H. ST. JOHN

Boston, Massachusetts
September 1974

Acknowledgments

Research for this book was begun during the years that I was on the faculty of the Harvard Graduate School of Education. It was made possible through the sponsorship of Dean Theodore Sizer, and of Harold Hunt and Vincent Conroy, then directors of the Administrative Career Program and Center for Field Studies. I am deeply grateful to them for their constant encouragement and for the financial support they arranged.

While the work was in progress I benefited greatly from the example, advice, and criticism of colleagues at Harvard. I am especially indebted to Nathan Glazer, Christopher Jencks, and Thomas Pettigrew. Others I thank for their ideas and interest are Robert Anderson, William Buss, David Cohen, Robert Dreeben, Neal Gross, Robert Herriott, Florence Ladd, Gerald Lesser, Marshall Smith, and William Spady.

Many of my students at Harvard (who are now for the most part the holders of Harvard doctorates) also contributed to my education on the topics discussed here. I especially valued my work with several whose research interests coincided with my own — Tom Boysen, Alonzo Crim, Roy Eikerenkotter, Toby Marotta, Robert Mathai, Milbrey McLaughlin, Edward McMillan, and Dorothy Uhlig. Among those who very kindly critiqued early drafts of chapters were Florence Davidson, Barbara Jackson, Sara Lightfoot, Michael Olney, Roger and Nancy Riffer, Paul Smith, and Elizabeth Useem. Mary Guttmacher and Eva Traves lent their expertise and enthusiasm as research assistants. My warmest thanks to each of these dear friends.

The book was largely written during the years 1971–1973 while I was a Fellow of the Radcliffe Institute. I extend very special thanks to the staff of the Institute and particularly to Alice Smith, Doris Lorentzen, and Janet Giele for providing so supportive, serene, and stimulating a setting in which to work. Nancy Santa Luca played a central role in the final stages of the study, relentlessly tracking elusive references, checking the accuracy of the charts, and translating endless drafts into polished form. Each page reflects her loving care.

I am grateful to the editors of *The American Educational Research Journal* and *Integrated Education* and to the Jossey-Bass Publishing Company for permission to use material from papers published by them.

With continuing awareness of his part in the work, I inscribe this book to Jim St. John. His interest in race relations and full opportunities for black Americans was the impetus that took us to Fisk University for seven years and stirred my interest in these topics. His understanding of the task of schools and the needs of youth schooled me. And his encouragement gave me the freedom to become a sociologist and to study desegregation from that perspective.

N. H. St. J.

Contents

School Desegregation

1. The Subject Defined

1. FOCUS ON CHILDREN

School desegregation has been a major social movement and source of continued national and local conflict in the third quarter of the twentieth century in the United States. This book deals with a partial but vital aspect of the process—its consequences for children.

The focus on consequences for children should be stressed at the outset. The subject here addressed is not the constitutional or moral necessity for racial desegregation of public schools, which both appear self-evident to me. Nor is this a historical analysis of local decision-making through identification of the protagonists, their tactics, or the variables affecting the speed, sequence, and nature of the steps taken to eliminate segregation. Ignored too will be the outcomes for nation and city—gains or losses in the political and economic development of the black community, in the racial understanding and attitudes of the white community, or in moral integration and racial harmony between blacks and whites. These are all matters that deserve (and have received) serious study, but they are not the topics of this book.

The question to be treated in the chapters that follow is narrower: What is the effect of racial mixing in school on the children involved? On balance does it benefit them? There are those who argue that benefits for children are of secondary importance in view of the constitutional and moral imperative that segregation in all forms be eliminated. In their opinion even if desegregation confers no blessing or is indeed a hardship to the youth of this generation, it is nevertheless justified if it furthers national unity or the ultimate achievement of a more just and egalitarian society. Others believe that only good means can lead to good ends and that the welfare of youth today is essential for the welfare of all tomorrow.

Phrasing the question differently may satisfy those in both camps. If, instead of posing a global question, we ask a precise question—In what ways and in what settings does desegregation benefit or harm children and how do children differ from one another in their response?—we may discover how to serve both individual children and society at large, both this generation and later generations.

These questions, important though they may seem, have not been the object of sustained public attention nor the best thinking of social scientists. In the political storm released by the 1954 Supreme Court decision, children often seemed forgotten, and in the decade that followed few empirical tests were undertaken of the Court's dictum that segregation is per se harmful to them.

Then came the Equality of Educational Opportunity report (Coleman et al., 1966). The magnitude of this study as well as the unexpectedness of its findings was a great stimulus to research on the school progress of minority children. The next eight years saw voluminous critiques of its methodology and conclusions, extensive reanalysis of its data, and a spate of smaller and more localized studies of the effects of desegregation. Though often uninformed by theory and methodologically imperfect, nevertheless these investigations together represent a tremendous investment in time, money, and print. It is time to take stock and ask what solid findings or important trends have been revealed.

At this particular point in time stock taking could be especially valuable. Judicial interpretation of the constitutional mandate for desegregation has expanded steadily. Most southern school systems have desegregated very recently and are still in the process of working out ways and means. And it appears likely that, in spite of the July, 1974, Supreme Court decision in regard to Detroit, metropolitan areas in the North will also experience large-scale desegregation. If twenty years of research has netted any collective wisdom on how children fare in biracial schools, that wisdom should be applied in the implementation phase that is ahead.

2. NARROWING THE FOCUS

What Is Desegregation? This book treats the consequences for children of the racial desegregation of their schools. But the subject needs further specification. First, what is a racially desegregated school? Many definitions have been proposed. According to one it is any school that is open to all children regardless of race. An alternative definition is based on the proportion of majority or minority group children enrolled. Although a school with one black child may be called desegregated, most definitions are more realistic, specifying for instance that not more than 90% of the pupils be of one race or that not more than 50% be minority group members.

A third approach rejects fixed quotas and suggests that the ethnic composition of a school should reflect the ethnic composition of the nation, state, or local community. A desegregated school is thus a "racially balanced" school, one in which there is proportionate representation of each racial group. Some insist on an exact match between school and community; others propose a tolerable range in ratios. For instance, the Dentler and Elkins (1967) formula is that no group in a school should be more than twice or less than half its proportion in the community. Delimiting the relevant community is a further issue. If the proportion black in the central city is such that racial balance would result in majority black schools, balance must be calculated and achieved on a metropolitan basis if schools are to be majority white.

Exact definition of segregation and desegregation may be necessary for legislatures, courts, or school boards, but a consideration of the outcomes of school racial composition for children should not be narrowly limited to any one part of that spectrum. This book, therefore, reviews all studies that examine the effect on pupils of their school's racial composition. In some studies a continuous variable, the school's percentage of pupils of one race or the other, is the independent variable. More frequently pupils in a "desegregated" or "racially balanced" school are compared with those in a "segregated" or "imbalanced" school, but the definitions of these terms vary considerably from study to study. A desegregated school may be simply one that enrolls pupils of more than one race, one that has recently changed from being one-race to being biracial, or one that is racially balanced according to some criterion. Though racial change, ratio, and balance thus do not narrow our consideration of desegregation, they are important conditions whose effects must be considered.

In this book, unless the context indicates a more specific meaning, desegregation encompasses all of these meanings; it is used to refer broadly to racial mixing in schools. The term "integration" often is used either interchangeably with desegregation or to refer to the condition that automatically follows the process of desegregation. I prefer, however, to follow the suggestion of Pettigrew (1971) and to reserve the term for that biracial situation in which the minority group is accepted on a completely equal basis. To avoid using the term integration unless there is evidence that the races meet on such terms may be stylistically awkward, but it reminds writer and reader of an important distinction. I shall discuss the distinction at greater length in Chapter 5.

Desegregation comes about in many ways. It may occur "naturally" in racially mixed neighborhoods or it may be planned to eliminate *de jure* or *de facto* segregation by school boards acting either spontaneously or in response to a court order or to community pressure.[1] It may be accomplished through the selective closing or building of schools, through redistricting, pairings, or busing. This study is concerned with the results for children, regardless of why or how desegregation is accomplished. But local variations in surrounding circumstances may condition the outcome and, like racial ratios, must therefore be studied as variables of potential significance.

Many investigations of school desegregation measure pupils' exposure to peers of another race at one point in time, whereas such exposure may vary considerably from year to year. Such discrepancy is particularly likely at the seventh or ninth grade as pupils move from elementary to secondary school. In addition, between-city and within-city migration of families means that many children attend several elementary schools, not all necessarily equally balanced or imbalanced racially. In many northern cities children who entered a mostly white school in first grade may find that same school mostly black six years later. Any study, therefore, which does not measure the independent variable longitudinally and accurately may miss important sources of variation in achievement and thus fail to demonstrate a relationship that in fact exists.

There is also the question of whether the important variable is school or classroom racial composition. Desegregated schools often practice within-school segregation. Homogeneous grouping or the assignment to classrooms on the basis of test scores or program usually results in considerable racial imbalance, rendering it virtually impossible to measure the effect of classroom race on achievement. Instead, achievement has affected classroom race. Hence, most researchers, although recognizing that the impact of racial mix may be greater at the classroom level, decide to measure it at the school level.

To repeat, school or classroom racial composition is the independent variable that here interests us. The studies reviewed in subsequent chapters compare in some fashion the effect on pupils of desegregation (or racial mixing in schools) with the effect of segregation (or racial separation in schools).

Desegregation of Whom? Where? When?   To turn from specification of the independent variable to specification of the sample, this book focuses on the effects of racial coeducation on blacks and whites, though much of the evidence and argument is relevant to the mixing of other ethnic groups. The grade levels that chiefly concern us are elementary and secondary, although some reference is made to studies of racial mixing in preschool or college.

The studies reviewed here were made in cities large and small and in all regions of the United States. One important empirical question is whether city size or region places a condition on the relationship between school racial composition and measures of its effect. It should be noted that the studies I conducted were located in three cities in the Northeast. Thus the analysis and argument in final chapters that deal with theory and policy may reflect this regional bias and seem less relevant to the situation in the Deep South.

To study the effect of racially mixed schools on children *now* or in the coming decade, we must use the evidence of studies

conducted over the past two decades. Such evidence is potentially misleading or irrelevant, for the meaning of desegregation
in 1974 or 1984 may be different from what it was in 1954 or
1964. More important than date may be the stage, in the
demographic and political history of a city, at which a study is
undertaken. The growth of the local black population in either
numbers or consciousness of its own power could affect both
the course and impact of desegregation.

The national mood has changed since 1954 in one important
respect. The Black Revolt has engendered disillusionment with
civil rights and waning interest in desegregation on the part of
many black leaders and citizens. For them, racial integrity,
self-determination, and political control of the communities and
institutions that affect their lives have replaced integration as top
priorities. In this connection it is worth noting that black social
scientists are conspicuously absent among researchers who measure the effects of school desegregation. This is a loss, for their
contribution might well involve asking more relevant questions
about the desegregation process and about its effect on students'
racial identification, militancy, and political self-consciousness.

What Outcomes?   This brings us to the question of what outcomes of school desegregation are here examined. Unfortunately, the range of variables that have been studied is limited to
three main areas: academic growth measured by standardized
achievement tests; motivation and self-confidence measured
through interviews, questionnaires, and a variety of instruments;
and interracial attitude and behavior measured by tests of social
distance or stereotyping, by sociometry, or by observation of
the incidence of conflict, cleavage, or friendly interaction. In
the next three chapters I define these variables and review the
evidence in regard to each. Chapter 2 reviews studies of academic achievement, Chapter 3 studies of motivation and self-
confidence, and Chapter 4 studies of interracial attitude and
behavior.

3. CHOICE OF RESEARCH DESIGN

Investigations of the effects of racial mixing in schools vary greatly in methods and procedures. The most serious methodological weakness is failure to meet the requirements of experimental design. To establish a causal relationship between school racial composition and academic performance, a researcher should employ the classic four-celled model with subjects randomly selected and assigned to experimental and control groups. Both groups should be tested before the experimental group is subjected to the test condition (i.e., racially mixed schools), and all other conditions should remain the same for both groups until they are tested again. A greater change between time 1 and time 2 for the experimental than the control group can then presumably be attributed to the effect of interracial schooling.[2]

Such experimental research in the area of desegregation is very difficult to achieve in practice. Policy-makers are in a hurry for results and urge a cross-sectional design in which children of segregated or desegregated schools are compared in time 2, without a time 1 measurement. Or if a longitudinal design is attempted, the random assignment to control and experimental conditions usually seems politically unfeasible and morally questionable. So all children in a desegregating system or the volunteers for a busing program are measured before and sometime after the onset of the experience, without comparing their gains with those of an appropriate control group of segregated children. Those using either type of two-celled design, whether cross-sectional or longitudinal, often try to simulate a four-celled experiment through statistical, rather than actual, control of other variables. But any correlation then found between key variables cannot be taken as evidence of a causal relation between them.

Equivalence of student inputs and of school treatments are the two factors most likely to contaminate research on the effect of racial segregation on the performance of children. Cross-sectional studies are plagued by the first difficulty—establishing that segregated and desegregated subjects were originally alike. Longitudinal studies are plagued by the second problem, since desegregation usually involves simultaneous changes in aspects of schooling other than racial composition.

Equivalence of Subjects.   In desegregation research the proper comparison is not between blacks and whites but within each racial group between the segregated and the desegregated. That children of any racial group do not all arrive at school equally ready to learn is axiomatic. Regardless of the relative contributions to academic aptitude of genes, of home environment, or of the interaction of these two, their joint effect on school progress is powerful. The Coleman Report documented dramatically the already well-established relation between socioeconomic status and achievement. It is therefore essential to neutralize the influence of such differences, child to child and family to family, in order to isolate any school-level effect. This is especially necessary in that black families who live in integrated neighborhoods or who volunteer for a busing program usually are found to be of higher SES than black families in the ghetto or families who do not volunteer.[3]

The best assurance of original equivalence is random assignment to segregated and desegregated conditions and/or the prior matching of these groups on achievement and SES, together with rigid control on mortality of the original sample through withdrawals or substitution of subjects. *Retrospective* longitudinal studies can select in time 2 subjects for whom comparable time 1 data exist in order to match them statistically on prior achievement and other known variables. However, the original equivalence of the groups is not thus completely assured, and differences between them on unmeasured variables may still contaminate the findings. *Prospective* longitudinal studies may be similarly vulnerable if they equate subjects on achievement only and do not use random assignment or careful matching on other variables. A further problem is introduced if different testing instruments are used for time 1 and time 2.

Equivalence of Schools.   Equivalence of school factors is rarely assured in desegregation research. Achievement growth between two points in time can be due to maturation, to differences in testing conditions, to factors in the community or nation, or to school variables other than the particular one a researcher is interested in measuring—in this case the influence of racial composition. A necessary component of an adequate research design is therefore a control group whose members experience all these conditions except that they remain in segregated schools. Unless testing conditions and community conditions are similar for the experimental and comparison groups, the gain or loss accompanying desegregation may be caused by factors other than racial mixing. Several of the studies reported here fail in this respect.

To isolate the racial composition factor, schools should be matched, just as individuals should be matched, on all relevant other characteristics. In pre-Coleman Report days probably few people doubted that school quality varied with racial composition, or that predominantly black schools were by and large inferior to predominantly white ones in physical plant, equipment, curricular offerings, and teacher qualifications. Comparisons of black and white schools in the South (McCauley and Ball, 1959) or ghetto and nonghetto schools in the North (Conant, 1961; Sexton, 1961) have until recently supported this conclusion. However, Coleman et al. (1966) found within regions surprisingly little difference between schools attended by majority and minority children and found moreover that those differences that did exist explained little of the between-school variation in achievement. Both of these findings have stood up under reanalyses of the Equality of Educational Opportunity (EEOS) data (Mosteller and Moynihan, 1972).

Thus there is some evidence that school quality may not be as serious a contaminating factor in school desegregation research as might have been thought, but it is possible that the EEOS, by using crude measures of school resources or by averaging scores across a large number of communities, has obscured real effects at the local level.[4] It would therefore be a wise precaution if researchers controlled on school quality as carefully as possible. Confining a study to a single school system gives some assurance that staffing, curriculum, and other policies are roughly similar in schools of various racial mixes, though it is probably impossible even within a single system to equate exactly the quality of schools serving different populations. Busing experiments in which children are transported from overcrowded ghetto to affluent suburban schools are in this respect especially poor tests of the influence of the racial factor alone. This does not mean that such experiments are without value as demonstrations of the viability and potential benefits of such mixing to all concerned. Children may benefit greatly from programs in which they are simultaneously exposed to changes in school quality and school race, even though researchers cannot thus determine which of these changes was the most beneficial.

To this point the discussion has assumed that majority-white schools may be superior to majority-black schools in subtle if not obvious ways, but the introduction of compensatory programs into most central city schools systems *may* have the opposite effect, though evidence to date does not so indicate. To the extent that such programs tend to remove former inequities and to equalize education across schools of different racial composition, they act as a control and make it more possible to test the effect of desegregation per se. To the extent that they go beyond equalization and offer *extra* services to segregated minority group children—newer buildings, smaller classes, greater per pupil expenditure, more highly prepared teachers—they could make it more rather than less difficult to demonstrate the benefit of desegregation.[5]

The social and economic (SES) background of peers is one school factor that is particularly hard to control in school desegregation research. Coleman (1966) and Wilson (1967) both found that, next to the influence of a pupil's own family background, the strongest influence on his achievement was the family background of his school peers. Moreover, once the SES of school peers was controlled, then race bore no relation to achievement. Confidence in the strength of the relationship between individual achievement and the SES of schoolmates has been somewhat shaken by reanalyses of the EEOS data by Smith (1972) and others which do not completely support this conclusion.

A major problem in the way of further attempts to control on this factor SES in desegregation research is the demographic pattern of our cities: though there are in increasing numbers middle-class black families, they do not yet exist in sufficient concentration to create genuinely middle-class, majority-black schools. Therefore, while we can compare the effect (for children who attend majority-white schools) of having schoolmates who are either lower class or middle class, we cannot compare the effect (for children who attend middle-class schools) of having schoolmates who are either mostly white or mostly black. If the school is middle class, it will rarely be mostly black. However, since a choice does currently exist between desegregation that crosses social class barriers and desegregation that does not, the analytic separation of these two types of desegregation is important. An important policy issue is involved.

What is the Comparison?   "What is the comparison?" is a key question in testing the effectiveness of a treatment. In cross-sectional studies of achievement we compare scores, and in longitudinal studies we compare gains. In four-celled studies we compare the gains of the desegregated with the gains of the segregated. The designer of a longitudinal study in a totally desegregated school system has no completely appropriate control group and must choose among four alternative comparison groups. The annual gain of a group of pupils in a biracial school can be compared with the annual gain in a former one-race school, either of this same group of pupils when in earlier grades or of a different group of students in the same grades. Or else the gain can be compared with that of local white children or with all children nationally (standardized norms).

The choice of relevant comparison group may seriously affect the researcher's conclusions. Chart 1-1 illustrates the problem. Let us arbitrarily assume a system in which, when desegregation begins (time 1), local white children are somewhat above national norms and black children are somewhat below those same norms. In the period that follows (time 1 to time 2) desegregated black children may improve relative to national norms, but the interpretation of this gain depends on the concurrent performance of other children in the system. In situation A desegregation appears clearly beneficial to black children, and in situation B it is beneficial to both black and white children, even though the gap between them in this case does not close. But in situation C and D, the desegregated do not benefit relative to any contemporaneous local group of segregated children; the whole black community or the whole system apparently received a boost at the time of desegregation.

It is also possible for the desegregated to make no gains relative to national norms and yet to decrease the gap between their achievement and that of local white children (situation E and F), or to increase the gap between their achievement and that of segregated blacks (situations E and G). Without a control group of segregated black children, the researcher might report gains in situations C, D, and F, a conclusion that might be unwarranted. He might also fail to report gains in situations B and G unless he were wise and ascertained earlier trends for formerly segregated pupils, trends that might resemble those in sample H.

Chart 1-1 Hypothetical trends in achievement scores of desegregated black pupils relative to segregated blacks, local whites, and national norms

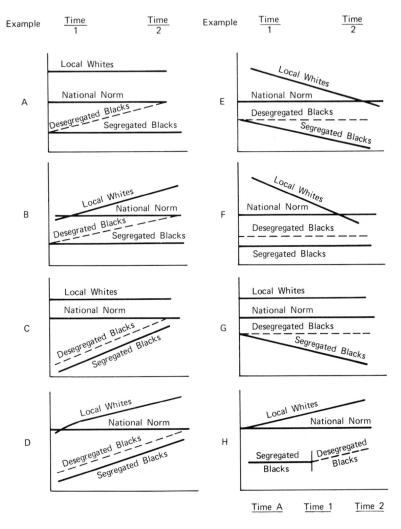

The reviews that follow attempt to specify which type of comparison is built into the design of each study and to evaluate its findings accordingly.

NOTES

1. For a discussion of "natural desegregation" cf. Dentler and Elkins (1967).

2. See Campbell and Stanley (1963) for a full treatment of the difficulties of experimental or quasi-experimental designs in educational research.

3. Several studies of open enrollment decision-making report a positive relationship between social indicators and choice of integrated schools (Saenger, 1961; Weinstein and Geisel, 1962; Chesler and Segal, 1967; Hartnett, 1970 [at the college level]; and Binderman, 1972). However, two other studies found no such relationship (Crockett, 1957; and Cagle and Beker, 1968), and in a third community it was lower- rather than middle-class black parents who elected integration for their children (Luchterhand and Weller, 1965).

4. See Spady (1972) on inadequacies of EEOS measures of school quality. Pettigrew et al. (1973) note that in a number of communities educational services were *decreased* with the onset of desegregation, hence concealing possibly significant positive desegregation effects.

5. A recent HEW (Lynn, 1972) review of the evidence concludes that, contrary to previous reviews of the topic (Gordon and Wilkerson, 1966; U.S. Commission on Civil Rights, 1967a), *focused* compensatory programs have been generally effective the nation over. See Jencks et. al. (1972c) and Clark (1973) for alternative views on equality of schooling.

"School marks are very important to me because they mean getting promoted and going to college." (black girl, grade 6)

"What seems to me really unfair is that I'm not smart" (black boy, grade 9)

"When I look in the mirror I see a failure" (white boy, grade 9)

"School marks are stupid just because some kids were borned stupid its not their fault and they get killed when they come home" (white girl, grade 6)

2. Desegregation and Academic Achievement[1]

1. MEASUREMENT OF ACHIEVEMENT

Do desegregated black children read or subtract better than segregated black children?

Does black growth in verbal skill accelerate over time in racially mixed schools?

Does the achievement of white children decline if black children are bused to their schools?

Does the black-white gap in mean test scores tend to close following the desegregation of a school system?

Questions such as these, which reflect the hopes of integrationists and the fears of segregationists, have preoccupied those engaged in studying the effects of school desegregation. Academic achievement may be a multidimensional concept, but its operational definition tends to be one- or two-dimensional. Many possible outcomes of schooling—creativity, curiosity, civic responsibility, moral judgment, artistic taste, leadership skill, human sensitivity, to name a few—however important, typically go unmeasured in educational research. Therefore, though the subject of this chapter could be the relation of school racial composition to children's total intellectual, artistic, and social development, I can report only research that treats verbal or mathematical skill as the measure of achievement.

In most studies of the outcome of desegregation the criterion is the raw or grade-equivalent score on a standardized achievement test (or composite score on a battery of such tests). In a few studies "mental ability" or "scholastic aptitude" or IQ is the criterion variable, whereas in others mental ability or IQ is used as a control when estimating achievement in reading or arithmetic. There are serious problems in the use of either type of test in desegregation research. If the tests have not been standardized and validated on a similar population (and they rarely have), they may have low predictive validity for black children or differentiate poorly among them.[2] Though the comparison is between black children and other black children, rather than between black and white children, the tests may nevertheless show unreliable or unreal differences or fail to show differences that are reliable and real.

Beyond this there is the further question of whether IQ should be used as a control in estimating differences in achievement. As long as IQ was considered fixed at birth and immune to the effects of environment, it seemed reasonable to focus on "achievement" within the limits set by "ability" in any study of the outcomes of different types of schooling. The contemporary shift in outlook of psychologists to the view that intelligence is plastic and the product of the interaction of genetic and environmental factors means that we can expect differences in school environment to result in differences in performance on

IQ tests, as well as on tests which measure the results of instruction in skills. Controlling on the results of a contemporaneous IQ test therefore may make it difficult to detect differences in achievement between experimental and control group. The difficulty is especially great in the case of children of any minority subculture.

Studies in which IQ is controlled are not the rule in desegregation research and their findings can thus be discounted. On the other hand it is not possible to ignore all studies that depend on the evidence of standardized achievement tests. No better criteria are generally available. The consequent uncertainty as to the meaning of their findings in regard to minority group children must be kept constantly in mind.

The experimental model discussed in the previous chapter suggests a logical way of classifying research on the relation of school racial composition and academic achievement. The ideal design provides for measurement in four cells:

	Before	After
Experimental Group	(1) Segregated	(3) Desegregated
Matched Control Group	(2) Segregated	(4) Segregated

But in many designs one or more of these cells are empty. I will first review cross-sectional studies that lack prior measurement of achievement, then longitudinal studies that lack a proper control group, and finally studies with before and after data for both control and experimental groups. Such four-celled studies are quasi experiments rather than true experiments, in that the two samples are rarely randomly drawn or randomly assigned to segregated or desegregated schools, nor is there precision matching of the groups on home background or school quality. Moreover, the early measurement is in many cases determined post facto. Black children are the focus of the discussion that follows. A later section summarizes evidence on the effect of the racial composition of schools on white children.

2. A NATIONAL CROSS-SECTIONAL STUDY

The most important source of cross-sectional data for the comparison of segregated and nonsegregated school children is the Equality of Educational Opportunity Survey (EEOS). Since the findings by the authors of the original report[3] and of *Racial Isolation in the Public Schools*[4] have been widely disseminated and argued and since the data have been subjected to careful reanalyses by many social scientists,[5] I will not discuss the matter here. But to set these studies in their rightful place in this review of school desegregation research, I must summarize briefly those findings of the original and subsequent analyses that are most relevant to the topic of this chapter and note those methodological limitations that inevitably affect our acceptance of such findings.

The Coleman Report stated that the proportion white in a school was positively related to individual performance, but that the "effect appeared to be less than, and largely accounted for, by other characteristics of the student body than the racial composition of the school per se" (i.e., by their SES). The Commission on Civil Rights' reanalysis of the data for twelfth-grade black students in the metropolitan northeast and ninth-grade blacks in eight regions indicated that the racial composition of the classroom in the previous year did have an independent relationship to students' verbal achievement. As suggested in the previous chapter, however, if pupils are assigned to classrooms on the basis of test scores, the direction of causality may not be from classroom percentage white to achievement, as assumed by the commission. On the other hand, in support of their assumption, the commission found that the earlier the grade at which blacks first reported having white classmates, the higher their achievement.

Further analysis of the EEOS data by McPartland (1968) agrees with the commission's conclusion on the relation between classroom composition and achievement. He shows that school desegregation is associated with higher achievement for black pupils only if they are in predominantly white classrooms, but classroom desegregation is favorable irrespective of school percentage white. The classroom racial composition effect, says McPartland, is not entirely explained by selection into track or curriculum.

A reanalysis by Cohen, Pettigrew, and Riley (1972) reaffirms the Coleman finding that the racial composition of the schools has little effect on the verbal achievement of blacks when school quality and the background of individuals and their peers are controlled. But, as the commission and McPartland had earlier reported, the racial composition of the classroom does have a modest relationship to verbal achievement (not apparently purely a result of selection processes) even after controlling for the foregoing factors. "A moderate proportion of the variance attributed to school social class is, in fact, shared with school percent Negro, and cannot be uniquely decomposed into either its racial composition or social-class components" (Cohen et al., 1972, p. 347).

Regardless of the finesse of the several analyses of the EEOS data, the following major criticisms of the quality of those data suggest that any conclusions as to the influence of school race on children must be considered tentative:

1. Without prior measures of academic performance there is no assurance that segregated and integrated children were comparable in scholastic aptitude when they entered these schools.[6]

2. The measures of home background are of doubtful validity and certainly do not measure or control on all facets of family influence.

3. School and classroom percentage white refer to one point in time and may not be accurately reported.

4. In spite of the many school characteristics measured in the survey, the quality of schooling in respects other than racial mixture is probably inadequately controlled. Failure to match teachers and their own pupils or to allocate per pupil expenditure by schools are among the sources of slippage.

Each of these could mask an actual relationship between school race and pupil achievement. If pupils are coded as "integrated" (though they had just arrived that week in a mixed school after eight years of segregation) or as "middle class" (though they are in fact from poverty-level homes), or as the recipients of "quality" schooling (though actually their class had a series of poorly trained substitutes all last year), then their low test scores coupled with "integration," "middle-class status," or "equal school resources" would diminish the apparent relation between integration and achievement for the group of which they were a part.

3. LOCAL CROSS-SECTIONAL STUDIES

The Equality of Educational Opportunity Survey was not the first cross-sectional study which, without the benefit of baseline data, compared the school achievement of segregated and desegregated black children. Chart A-1 (in the Appendix) lists 13 other such studies, all at the local rather than national level. This listing, like similar ones to follow, includes all published and unpublished studies of the specified type that I have found reported in sufficient detail to allow classification. Though my search has been long and hard, I undoubtedly have missed some relevant research.[7]

It is probably no accident that most of these studies were initiated before the release of the Coleman Report in 1966. That important document demonstrated so clearly the need for longitudinal data that few subsequent investigators have failed to incorporate some "before" as well as "after" measurement into their research designs. It is also noteworthy that the studies (in at least nine different northern states from Connecticut to California) all had small samples and compared the achievement of "naturally" desegregated and segregated pupils. In other words, racially mixed schools were the result of demographic changes in school districts, not of deliberate action on the part of school boards, a feature also symptomatic of the era in which the data were gathered.

Differences in social and economic status between the segregated and the desegregated were controlled in some fashion in most of these investigations, but it is doubtful that the two groups were thereby equated in family background. The only two researchers who reported unmixed findings of significantly higher achievement for the integrated (Jessup, 1967; Lockwood, 1966) had very little control on family background.

Several studies treated IQ as a control rather than as another measure of the outcome of desegregation. As noted, this presents a problem of interpretation. If the IQ test is contemporaneous with the reported achievement score, then to "remove its effect" may reduce not merely the initial difference between groups, as these researchers assume, but also the hypothesized relation between the race of classmates and achievement. The findings of no significant difference between the two groups of children tested reported by several researchers (Crowley, 1932; Long, 1968; Robertson, 1967) or the mixed findings reported by other researchers (Matzen, 1965; Samuels, 1958) may be artifacts of this procedure.

Chart A-1 summarizes four cross-sectional studies (in Chicago, Pittsburgh, Plainfield, and New Haven) that measured school race longitudinally. In each case secondary or postsecondary school achievement was the criterion and earlier desegregation experience the predictor. In these studies the previously integrated tended to outperform the previously segregated, but the controls were not stringent, nor were the differences reported to be large or statistically significant, with the exception of the Pittsburgh study.

Since the Pittsburgh study which I conducted (St. John, 1973) is a good example of the problems of interpreting the results of such research, I will describe it in some detail. Eight of the 21 secondary schools in that city were selected as representative of the schools attended by minority group students in 1966. The 1388 black ninth graders in those schools were 72% of the black ninth graders in the city and were graduates of 60 different elementary schools that varied considerably in their racial and social class composition. For each student I calculated the average percentage of white students and the average social class level of the schools he had attended in grades 1 to 8.

Pupils' elementary school percentage white (which ranged from 0 to 99%) was the independent variable in subsequent tabular and regression analyses and proved to be positively and significantly related to eighth-grade Metropolitan Achievement Test score in arithmetic. The relationship did not disappear either when sex and family SES were controlled or when boys and girls or students of high and low SES and IQ were analyzed separately. However, other achievement test scores (in reading, language, or science) were not related to school percentage white, though they were related to school SES.

The results of the Pittsburgh analysis are thus ambiguous: desegregation apparently encouraged skill in arithmetic but not in other subjects. One possible explanation for this discrepancy is that arithmetic in contrast to reading is a school-learned skill and was perhaps better taught in racially mixed schools. Another possible explanation is that segregated and desegregated students were not originally alike in their potential for learning arithmetic. Without random assignment, matching, or a pretest, it is impossible to determine the reason for the difference in results.

The other cross-sectional studies suffer from the same weakness, but since a strong relationship between integration experience and achievement was seldom found, there is little danger of a spurious conclusion. Only if the integrated were *less* advantaged than the segregated could their gains be greater and their final scores the same. Given the usual demography of cities, such a possibility is unlikely. It is in connection with the few studies in this group that find the desegregated significantly ahead that the question of inadequate controls and possible spuriousness must be seriously considered.

Longitudinal Studies. The last few years have seen an increase in studies that have the benefit of before and after measurement of achievement but lack a genuine control group. Fourteen such studies are listed in Chart A-2, in three southern and five northern states from East to West Coast, plus the District of Columbia. In most cases the studies followed total district desegregation; therefore the samples were fairly large and no contemporary control group of segregated peers was possible. The duration of the study was only one year in the case of five of these reports, from two to five years in the others. The focus of most of the studies was the elementary level. The busing of black children was a feature of the desegregation plan in most of these studies, but only in Boston were black children transported out of the city to suburban schools.

Few of these studies reported clear gains for desegregated minority group children in comparison with national norms, local whites, or their own previous growth in a segregated setting. Methodological problems detracted from the Washington, D.C., and Louisville findings. Systemwide desegregation did not mean desegregated classes for most children in these cities at the time of the studies. No tests of statistical significance were reported for Berkeley, but trends there did not favor the desegregated. No consistently significant gains were reported for White Plains, Evanston, or Riverside. In several other cities findings were mixed, with significant gains in some subjects but not others or at some grade levels but not others. The most clear-cut positive findings were those in Hoke County and Goldsboro, North Carolina, where blacks showed post-desegregation gains relative to national norms.

In none of these longitudinal studies was individual family background measured or controlled, though this may not be a serious limitation if the sample includes all children in the system. However, it is probable that the classmates of black children were of higher average SES after desegregation than before and that any relative growth that occurred might have been due to this factor as much as to school race. It is also probable that desegregation meant changes for the better in school quality for the black children involved. There is good evidence that in Washington, D.C., and Louisville, for instance, major systemwide educational improvements accompanied desegregation. However, in some cities (e.g., in Berkeley, according to a study by Frelow, 1971), there was a reduction in services in the years following desegregation.

The Riverside experiment in desegregation is the most long-term, completely documented, and widely noted study in this group, and its findings are therefore particularly discouraging. In 1965 the school board voted a phased closedown of three very imbalanced elementary schools involving the busing of 225 pupils (47% black and 53% Mexican-American) to 17 other schools in the city. In their February 1973 report, Purl and Dawson summarized the findings after seven years of desegregation:

1. The achievement of kindergarten and first-grade minority students rose steadily and significantly and in 1972 was near the median of the norming sample. Second graders showed no trend and third graders decreased slightly.

2. Receiving pupils showed trends similar to those of bused pupils. Thus the gap between bused and receiving pupils narrowed only slightly.

3. The authors suggest that the gains in the first two years were the result of instructional improvement and greater individualization of classes. In the higher grades low achieving pupils showed the least progress and the need for compensatory programs.

4. Pupils attending certain schools consistently scored high or low. Sometimes the SES of receiving pupils and sometimes the quality of the instructional program seemed to be responsible.

Thus the gains of the younger children in Riverside might not be lost in the older grades if services were maintained at predesegregation levels and if minority group children were all allocated to classrooms in which the achievement level was high. But as it stands neither the Riverside evidence nor that of any of the other longitudinal studies provides strong support for the hypothesis that desegregated schooling benefits minority group children.

4. QUASI-EXPERIMENTAL FOUR-CELLED STUDIES

The last group of studies to be considered are four-celled, in that the achievement of segregated and desegregated subjects is measured at two points in time. These studies are quasi experiments rather than true experiments since subjects are neither assigned randomly from a common population to segregated or desegregated schools nor matched on all relevant variables. The presumed validity of their findings, although greater than that of two-celled studies, is not beyond question. Chart A-3 lists 37 such studies.

The dates of these reports range from 1958 to 1972, clustering in the late 1960s. The locations are New York state for 10, other northeastern cities for 9, with the others well distributed across the nation. Eleven samples had less than 50 black pupils in the experimental group, while five had over 1000; the modal size was between 100 and 500 desegregated black children. The great majority (29) were at the elementary level.

In most of these experiments, as compared to those with a longitudinal design, desegregation was not systemwide and mandatory for all. For research purposes this situation is useful, in that a control group of segregated children was thus available, but it also poses a serious research hazard, in that most of the desegregated were in one way or another self-selected. The desegregated were either children whose families chose an integrated neighborhood or, in most cases, those who volunteered for open enrollment or a busing program. Careful matching of subjects in the control and experimental groups on family background as well as early achievement was therefore essential. But such matching was rare, and only 11 studies made any attempt to control on socioeconomic status.

Two ways of handling the choice of control group are especially promising. The METCO studies reported by Walberg (1969) and Armor (1972a) tested segregated siblings of the pupils bused out to suburban schools and found that bused pupils did not show significantly greater gains than their brothers or sisters. Unfortunately, due to nonresponse the sample of siblings was too small and nonrandom to constitute an adequate control group. Project Concern reported by Mahan (1968) randomly selected whole classrooms to be bused to Hartford suburbs. Though a few parents refused this opportunity, such a precedure insured a large measure of comparability between experimental and control groups. In the younger grades (K to 3) bused Hartford pupils made significantly greater gains in IQ and achievement than pupils who remained in the city. In grades 4 to 6 the difference in achievement favored the segregated.

Another interesting feature of the Hartford study is that half of the receiving suburban classrooms were assigned extra ''supporting'' teachers. Greater gains were reported for pupils in these classrooms than for bused pupils without such support. On the other hand, there was no evidence that such assistance benefited pupils who remained in the inner city. The chief drawback of this project as a scientific experiment is, of course, the fact that the effects of racial composition and quality of schools are completely confounded.

The Wilson Study.   Among studies of the effect of "natural" or unplanned desegregation on minority group performance, the one with the most nearly adequate design is Wilson's (1967) survey, reported in an appendix to the Civil Rights Commission Report. The sample is a stratified random sample of over 4000 junior and senior high school students in one school district in the San Francisco Bay area. The design is a cross-sectional comparison of verbal test scores, according to the racial and social class composition of neighborhoods and schools, but retrospective longitudinal control is introduced by the data on school racial and social class composition at each grade level, and by the availability of first-grade individual mental maturity test scores. Wilson argues that controlling on these test scores equates children on the effects of both genetic differences and preschool home environment, so that changes can be attributed to new (school?) experiences and not to uncontrolled initial differences. I do not share Wilson's faith in the early test score.

Though the sample is large ($N = 905$ blacks in crucial tables), analysis of the separate effects of neighborhood and school segregation or of racial and social class segregation is hampered for blacks by the confounding of these variables and by the fact that few blacks live in integrated neighborhoods, thus seriously reducing the number of cases in some cells. Nevertheless, by means of regression analysis, Wilson showed that after controlling for variation in first-grade IQ and for parental and neighborhood SES, the social class of the primary school had a significant effect on sixth-grade reading level and the social class of the intermediate school a significant effect on eighth-grade verbal reasoning scores. School racial composition, however, had no significant effect on achievement over and above school social class (pp. 180-184).

Beyond the small size of the numbers in some of the cells, there are further limitations to this study:

1. First-grade scores would have been available only for the most stable members of the sample, and its representativeness may have been affected by attrition.

2. Children were matched only by father's occupation and primary mental maturity scores; in other respects segregated and integrated children could have been quite different.

3. Parental and school social class assignment based on the questionnaire replies of students are potentially inaccurate.

4. No evidence is offered as to the equality of segregated and integrated schools in Richmond.

5. If the relation between school racial composition and achievement was not linear, the regression analysis could have underestimated the effect.

But in spite of these quibbles, the study is impressive in design and quite convincing that in this community, at least, racial integration per se was not significantly related to the academic performance of blacks. But, given the strong intercorrelation of school racial and social class composition ($r \pm .77$), the combined effect of the two types of segregation was plainly a strong deterrent to achievement.[8]

The Goldsboro Study. A most interesting study of planned total district desegregation in a southern community is that by Mayer et. al. (1973) and McCullough (1972) of Goldsboro, North Carolina. Desegregation was accomplished there in a manner that equalized facilities, equipment, and staff for all pupils. Black schools were kept open and remodeled. All teachers were reassigned, and the principals of black schools became the principals of white schools and vica versa. Pupils were assigned by grade level rather than residence so that busing affected blacks and whites alike.

Longitudinal comparison was made of the third- and fifth-grade scores of a cohort of pupils who experienced systemwide desegregation between their third- and fourth-grade years. Both blacks and whites gained significantly relative to national norms in verbal and mathematical skills. The white-black gap, however, was not reduced. The authors suggest that desegregation may not have altered the status relationships between blacks and whites. Structured observations in fourth-grade classrooms revealed much less teacher-pupil intereaction of a substantive nature and much more interaction of a disciplining nature for black males than for white males.

A quasi-experimental design was then achieved by controlling on degree of desegregation experience. Pupils were classified according to the racial composition of their school in the year before systemwide desegregation and according to whether their school was desegregated in the first or second year of the experiment. In verbal achievement all groups made significant gains, with no significant differences according to desegregation experience. Apparently the fact of systemwide desegregation, not attendance at a desegregated school, boosted verbal achievement, since similar gains were experienced by those who remained at a segregated school in the fourth grade and by those who did not.

Achievement in arithmetic, on the other hand, *was* related to desegregation experience: black pupils who had longer experience in desegregated schools made significantly greater gains than the newly desegregated. The effect was not due to changes in teaching methods; a comparison of pupils experiencing open classroom teaching style with those who remained in traditional classrooms revealed that the latter made significantly greater improvement in arithmetic. Nor did social class alone account for the improvement, though the researchers did not examine possible intereaction between social class and desegregation experience.

The authors claim the effect of desegregation experience on mathematical but not verbal achievement occurs because "Social structural change is more likely to work in performance areas that are narrow and depend on recently acquired skills, than in performance areas that depend on more pervasive skills built up over a longer time period" (p. 42).

Chart 2-1 shows the frequency distribution of the 36 four-celled studies summarized in Chart A-3 according to the direction of their findings and whether SES was controlled and tests of significance reported. It is evident that the findings are partially or wholly positive much more frequently than they are negative. However, it is also evident that the tighter the design the more often is no difference found between segregated and desegregated minority group children. We therefore cannot ignore the possibility that positive findings would disappear completely in studies with more perfect control of all relevant variables.[9]

Space does not allow full description of each of these four-celled studies. Taken together, however, they suggest that the achievement of black children is rarely harmed thereby, but they provide no strong or clear evidence that such desegregation boosts their achievement. A countdown by grade level and achievement tests, rather than by cities, reveals that a report of no difference is more common than a report of significant gain. Even studies over several years are as often negative as positive in their findings. And where gains are established, we are left to wonder whether the effective agent was the quality of desegregated schools, the selection of the busing program by the children of mobility-oriented families, or contact with middle-class or white schoolmates.

Two findings already noted in connection with two-celled studies receive further support from four-celled studies: five of

Chart 2-1 Frequency Distribution of Four-celled Studies of Relation of Schools Racial Composition and Black Achievement, by Direction of Findings and by whether Design included Control on SES and Tests of Significance

Direction of Findings	No SES Control, No Test of Significance	No SES Control, Yes Test of Significance	Yes SES Control, Yes Test of Significance	Total
Positive on all tests reported	Banks and DiPasquale (1969) Dressler (1967) Heller et al. (1972) Johnson (1967)	Anderson (1966) Zdep and Joyce (1969)	Griffin (1969)	7
Mixed positive and negative or no difference	None	Beker (1967) Carrigan (1969) Clinton (1969) Fortenberry (1959) Laird and Weeks (1966) Mahan (1968) Mayer et. al., (1973) Rochester School Board (1970) Rock et al. (1968) Sacramento School Board (1971)	Frary and Goolsby (1970) Slone (1968) Walberg (1969) St. John and Lewis (1971)	18

No difference	Fox (1966, 1967, 1968)	Samuels (1971) Williams (1968) Wolman (1964) Wood (1969) Danahy (1971) Gardner et al. (1970) Moorefield (1967) Rentsch (1967)	Denmark and Guttentag (1969) Klein (1967) Laurent (1969) Wilson (1967)	9
Mixed no difference and negative	Shaker Heights (1972)	None	Armor (1972a) Evans (1969)	3
Negative on all tests reported	None	None	None	0
Total	7	19	11	37

these reports note that gains of desegregated black children are more evident in earlier than in later grades; and achievement in arithmetic but not reading was found to be significantly and positively related to school race in New York, Boston, and Goldsboro.[10] Both of these tendencies deserve further testing.

5. WHITE STUDENTS

Research on the effect of desegregation on school achievement has usually focused on minority group students, whereas research on the effect of prejudice has focused on white students. In the majority of the studies summarized above, the achievement of white students is either ignored entirely or else treated as the norm against which the gains of black students should be measured. But the prospect of reverse busing of white students to formerly black schools has stimulated interest in the probable effects on their academic progress. Chart A-4 summarizes 24 studies of the achievement of desegregated whites.

The Coleman et al. (1966) cross-sectional finding that school percentage white bears little relation to verbal achievement that is independent of the influenece of individual and school social background referred to white children as well as to minority group children. The U.S. Commission on Civil Rights Report (1967) reaches the same conclusion in regard to classroom rather than school racial composition.[11] Armor's (1972b) reanalysis of the Coleman data clearly shows that the verbal ability of white pupils in majority-black schools is as low or lower than that of black schoolmates. It is apparently not the school's racial composition but the low SES of such pupils (and perhaps that of their classmates as well) that seems to be primarily responsible for their low achievement.

Using longitudinal data, Wilson (1967) found that for white students as well as black students the racial composition of the school had a negligible effect but was confounded with social class composition, which had a significant effect. For whites in comparison with blacks, school social class was less related to achievement, and family social class was more related to achievement.

In contrast, I found that residence in racially changing neighborhoods in Boston was associated with lower test scores for white children. The greater the percentage of black classmates in earlier grades, the lower the later achievement of whites in arithmetic and reading, even with parental and school SES and a measure of early achievement controlled. Fifty percent black was an important boundary. White children who had attended majority-black schools scored considerably below those who had attended majority-white schools (St. John and Lewis, 1971).

The longitudinal data from desegregating school systems—Berkeley, Chapel Hill, Evanston, Goldsboro, Louisville, Riverside, Washington, D.C., White Plains—indicate in every case that racial mixture in the schools had no negative consequences for majority group pupils. In busing experiments in which selected central city children are transported to outlying communities the universal report also is no significant difference in achievement between children in classrooms that do or do not receive bused pupils (Buffalo, Denver, Hartford, Westport, Verona, West Irondequoit). It should be noted, however, that in almost all these experiments, white children remained in the majority in their schools and classrooms.

A few reports are available on the academic progress of white children bused to schools in the ghetto. In Shaker Heights white pupils in grades 4 and 6 who accepted reassignement to a majority-black school gained more than whites in the rest of the system. In Evanston self-selected white children bused to a formerly black school had scores above the norm. O'Reilly (1970) reports on two similar cases. One study in Queens, New York, found that white students transported to a majority-black school made less academic progress than white students who remained home (Wrightstone et al., 1966). In the other study of reverse busing in Rochester, New York, no significant differences between the two groups of white students were found except that fourth-grade students transferred to an inner city school made significantly higher scores on vocabulary and arithmetic achievement tests (Rock et al., 1968).

The evidence appears convincing that the achievement of white students is not adversely affected by the addition of a few black students to their classrooms. Classrooms over 50% black are quite possibly detrimental to white achievement, but this has been tested so little with longitudinal data that it remains an open question. The rare studies of reverse busing of suburban children to ghetto schools show gains more often than losses, but families who choose reverse busing may have unusual children.

6. CONCLUSION

In sum, adequate data have not yet been gathered to determine a causal relation between school racial composition and academic achievement. More than a decade of considerable research effort has produced no definitive positive findings. In view of the political, moral, and technical difficulties of investigation on this question, it is doubtful that all the canons of the scientific method will ever be met or a causal relationship ever established. Suggestive trends have been uncovered, however, as has one important negative finding: desegregation has rarely lowered academic achievement for either black or white children.

Light and Smith argue that "little headway can be made by pooling the words in conclusions of a set of studies. Rather progress will only come when we are able to pool, in a systematic manner, the original data from the studies" (1971, p. 343). Their argument is persuasive; but until such pooling can be accomplished we may learn something from noting the short-comings of existing studies and the direction of their findings.

The studies reviewed in this chapter were conducted in communities that range across the country and vary greatly in population. But there is no evidence that city size or region affects the influence of desegregation on achievement. The northern, middle-sized city was until recently the most frequent location because this is where desegregation was most possible and probable in the 1960s. Since 1970, however, a number of studies of southern school systems have appeared, but their findings are as mixed as those of northern systems.

Similarly, research has focused on the elementary grades because at this level neighborhood housing patterns have produced the greatest variation in school racial mixture. Here there is some indication that younger children, especially those of kindergarten age, tend to benefit more than older children from desegregation. The length of exposure to desegregation, however, has not so far proved to be an important variable, perhaps because most experiments or studies thereof have been of very short duration. A further cause for uncertainty in this regard is that childrens' total experience with school desegregation from kindergarten on is usually not measured at all or measured imprecisely.

When significant differences in favor of the desegregated are reported, in some but not all test, there is no consistency as to which academic skill is most affected. However, gains in mathematical rather than verbal achievement are reported frequently enough to deserve further study.

In the studies reviewed there is considerable variation in the definition of the independent variable. In most studies school racial composition rather than classroom racial composition is the focus, and reports do not specify whether grouping practices resulted in within-school desegregation. Since classroom race may be the result of grouping based on test scores, school race seems the preferable independent variable. But within-school desegregation should be measured and controlled.

The Coleman Report and a few of the other studies reviewed treat school racial composition as a continuous variable, but it is far more frequently treated as a nominal variable, with the scores of the same pupils being compared before and after "desegregation" or the scores of different pupils, either "segregated" or integrated," being compared. A "segregated" school is variously defined as majority-black (greater than 50%) or predominantly black (greater than 80% or 90%) or totally black. Similarly "integrated" or "desegregated" refers sometimes to a majority-white school, but more often to a predominantly white situation in which desegregation is "token." There is no clear evidence in this literature that findings depend on the definition of desegregation. Tabular analyses of the EEOS data (U.S. Commission on Civil Rights, 1967) suggest that in some regions or at some SES levels there is a curvilinear relationship between school or classroom percentage white and achievement, with lowest mean achievement for black pupils where that percentage is between 25 and 50. But this finding may be a function of incomplete control on SES and other factors. Further study is needed before we can be sure whether, as some researchers have found, both races perform better in schools at least 50% white or whether tokenism, either for whites in black schools or blacks in white schools, affects achievement adversely.

The desegregation referred to in these studies came about in at least four different ways: through "natural" demographic changes in residential neighborhoods; through school board rezoning of districts or closing of a segregated school and mandatory transfer of its pupils, with or without busing; through voluntary transfer of selected pupils to distant schools through open enrollment or busing; and through total district desegregation in which all children, white or black, are assigned to schools of similar racial mix. In this last case, black children are more frequently bused than are white children. We have seen that the method by which a community achieves desegregation largely determines what type of evaluation is technically possible. However, available evidence does not suggest that the method determines whether academic gains result, though the matter has not been studied systematically. In many cases of desegregation through redistricting, some children must walk and some must be bused to the new school. But in only one city, Evanston (Hsia, 1971), were the achievement gains of busers and walkers compared. In this case the busers gained more.

More serious than ignorance as to the most favorable black-white ratio or the most favorable method of achieving that ratio is lack of research evidence as to the conditions under which desegregation (however defined or achieved) benefits children. Researchers have not controlled on such variables as the level of community controversy over desegregation, the friendliness of white parents and students, the flexibility or prejudice of the staff, the content of curriculum, or the method of teaching. There is some evidence, however, that individualization of instruction and the provision of support services for students in need of remedial work is an important concomitant of desegregation.

In the introduction to this chapter the point was made that the twin challenges to desegregation research are assurance as to the original equivalence of segregated and desegregated pupils and the equivalence of their schooling in all respects other than interracial exposure. We have found that "no significant difference" between segregated and desegregated black children is the finding of over half of the most carefully controlled studies and of many more than half of the tests of the relationship, if subject matter areas and grade levels rather than communities are counted. The question then before us is: Is it likely that tighter control on the equivalence of pupils and treatments would change the verdict? Wherever desegregation is found to *benefit* minority group children we must assure ourselves that this is not a spurious finding. But where *no difference* is found, it is unlikely that tighter controls would reveal a relationship. Experience suggests that it is unlikely that the absence of effect is due to the *lower* initial ability or SES of the desegregated pupils or to the *lower* objective quality of desegregated schools. The research hazard is rather that the desegregated may be children of greater initial potential than the segregated and that desegregated schools will be superior on tangible criteria. On the other hand it is entirely possible, and unfortunately highly probable, that many desegregated schools are unfriendly, irrelevant, and unsupportive to black pupils. Without control on such intangible qualities of schools it is impossible to measure the contribution to achievement of their black-white ratios.

One further point in regard to the academic consequences of desegregation deserves consideration. Does the way we pose our research question place the burden of proof unfairly on the minority group rather than the majority group? Desegregation is supposed to benefit the achievement of black children, not white children. It is pronounced a success if black achievement rises but white achievement remains stationary; in other words, it is successful if the racial gap is reduced. Given the demonstrated importance of early childhood influences and the high correlation for children generally between early and late test scores, why should we expect only one aspect of school experience—racial mix—to have a pronounced effect on achievement and, what is more, on the achievement of one racial group only? Moreover, why do we continue to measure minority group children's progress in school with tests normalized on the population at large, tests which may reflect very poorly their own group strengths, interests, and priorities?

NOTES

1. This chapter is a revised and much expanded version of a paper that appeared in *Review of Educational Research,* Volume 40, February 1970.

2. See Fishman et al. (1964).

3. Coleman et al. (1966).

4. U.S. Commission on Civil Rights (1967).

5. For example, see Bowles and Levin (1968); McPartland (1968); Hanusheh (1969); Mayeske et al. (1972); Mosteller and Moynihan (1972); Armor (1972b).

6. Jencks and Brown (1972) use an ingenious method of controling for variations in initial ability among students sampled in the EEO survey. They compare first and sixth graders in the same elementary schools. They find that both black and white achievement rose (relative to national norms) in elementary schools 51 to 75% white. The effects in secondary schools were small but suggested that blacks gain more in schools 26 to 90% white.

7. The work of Weinberg (1970), O'Reilly (1970), and Pettigrew et al. (1973) were especially helpful in locating studies and are here gratefully acknowledged. All dissertations referred to have been read, usually on microfilm.

8. See O'Reilly (1970) for a careful and detailed critique of this study.

9. Pettigrew (1969) reasons that "soft research . . . strongly suggests that desegregation has sustained and marked effects on the achievement of Negro children" (p. 104) and therefore feels it is likely that "hard" research will support this evidence. I find, rather, that "soft" research tends to show little effect and am therefore less sanguine than he that hard research will reveal clear benefits unless the conditions under which desegregation normally occurs are changed.

10. Slone (1968); St. John and Lewis (1971); Mayer et. al., 1973).

11. See page 47 and Tables 8-3, 8-4, and 8-6 of *Racial Isolation in the Public Schools*.

3. Desegregation and Self-Confidence

1. THE PREDICTIONS OF SOCIAL SCIENTISTS

Chief Justice Earl Warren, in delivering the opinion of the Supreme Court in *Brown v. Board of Education,* May 17, 1954, stressed the psychological rather than the academic consequences of school desegregation:

> To separate them from others of similar age and qualifications solely because of their race generates a *feeling of inferiority* as to their status in the community that may affect their *hearts and minds* in a way unlikely ever to be undone. (Emphasis added)

The Brown decision was supported by a brief signed by 32 prominent social scientists and reported an earlier poll indicating that anthropologists, psychologists, and sociologists agreed overwhelmingly that "enforced segregation has [a] detrimental effect" (Deutscher and Chein, 1948).

In the years after 1954, social scientists frequently voiced expert opinions on the subject of school desegregation, both as members of professional societies and in their individual writings, and these opinions often referred to its psychological aspects. For instance, a group of Cornell sociologists undertook to summarize existing social science knowledge relevant to desegregation as a social process (Suchman, Dean, and Williams, 1958). Their monograph is concerned chiefly with sociological factors (SES, power, attitudes) and community characteristics that would impede or facilitate desegregation and lead to acquiescence or resistance or violence, but it also suggests the potentially powerful psychological effects of school desegregation:

> School desegregation is likely to have these effects on the minority group youths: a more direct and constructive outlet for hostility; a lowering of hypersensitivity and of the tendency to sense hostility and rebuff in the well-intentioned actions of out-group members; a diminution of avoidance, withdrawal, or submissiveness reactions; a greater sense of personal dignity; a rise in personal ambition; a greater confidence and respect for their own sub-group and a lowering of ambivalence about minority group membership; a greater confidence in the American Democratic Creed and moral order. Negro youths are likely to attain higher standards of academic proficiency and exert their capacities more fully after desegregation, because of increased morale, decreased self-hatred, and a fuller sense of sharing the American Dream. (P. 71)[1]

Ten years later, in a 1964 poll of one quarter of the American

Educational Research Association membership, the median respondent felt that attendance at mostly black schools has a *rather* negative effect on a Negro child's academic achievement but a *very* negative effect on his perception of his status in society, whereas attendance at a racially balanced school is favorable on both counts (Seasholes, 1965).

Individual social scientists also made predictions of the effects of desegregation, a number of which were very pessimistic. Three arguments predominated. Those who hold basically racist views as to the intelligence or learning style of Negroes hypothesized that both races would suffer from mixed schools.[2] Others expressed concern over the psychic tensions that desegregation was likely to engender for black children.[3] A third antidesegregation argument has been stressed by such writers as Handlin (1966), Carmichael and Hamilton (1967), and Piven and Cloward (1967), who believe that dissipation of the ghetto will result in loss of black identity and any chance of political effectiveness.[4]

Such antidesegregation pronouncements have been answered by social scientists who draw on knowledge of their disciplines or professional experience to develop opposite predictions. That blacks are inherently different from whites in academic potential or learning style is strenuously rejected by leading sociologists and psychologists.[5] Most scholars have therefore assumed (without much dissection of the causal mechanisms involved) that desegregation will expose blacks to a more stimulating academic environment and thus raise their achievement, self-confidence, and aspiration. As to the psychological hazards of desegregation for the black child, psychologists argue on the one hand that these have been grossly exaggerated[6] and on the other that stress will be less severe under desegregation than under continued segregation.[7] Desegregation is necessary to eradicate the heritage of the Southern caste system[8] or the Northern ghetto[9] and to arrest the movement toward two separate Americas which the National Advisory Commission on Civil Disorders (1968) decries.

Expert opinion as to the probable consequences of desegregation has tended to be strangely uncritical and ungrounded in theory. Indeed there seem to be real grounds for Metzger's (1971) charge that "the convergence of liberal and sociological thought in the area of race relations is striking and raises serious questions about the 'value-free' character of sociological inquiry in this area" (p. 269).[10]

When we turn from opinion to evidence, the contribution of social science to our understanding of the psychological effects of integration is still more baffling. Zirkel (1971), who recently reviewed a section of this literature concludes,

> The effects of ethnic group mixture in the school on the self-concepts of students is a subject that has evoked much heat but little light. . . .
>
> The seeming lack of consistency, clarity, and completeness in these research findings is no doubt due in large part to what Wylie (1961, p. 2) termed a "bewildering array" of definitions, instruments, and research designs. (Pp. 214, 216)

Such forewarnings are discouraging. However, the value of integrating the research on a topic of interest outweighs the possible problems. Only thus can we reap the benefit of scattered, intensive, small-scale studies, simulate replication of their findings, and achieve some cumulation of knowledge.[11]

In spite of the interest of social scientists in the topic, there have been many fewer empirical studies of the effects of biracial schooling on attitudes than of its effects on achievement. Schools are in the habit of making annual appraisals of student growth in academic skills, not in self-confidence or motivation. Thus the source of studies for this chapter is rarely the official report of a school system. Most studies seem to have been the work of professional educators rather than professional psychologists. The studies are more frequently reported in educational than in psychological journals, or they have been the subject of dissertations for the Ed.D. rather than for the Ph.D. in psychology.[12] It is unfortunate that the subject has not received more attention from psychologists as well, for adequate handling of the topic entails a high order of theoretical understanding and methodological skill.

Awareness of possible bias in the sampling of studies reviewed is essential. In Chapter 2 I stated that I had not uncovered every study of school desegregation and achievement; I repeat the disclaimer here. Included, however, are every study I found comparing the attitudes or personality traits of segregated or desegregated black youth or measuring a change in these respects following desegregation.[13] Nonquantitative anthropological or interpretive descriptions that do not make such comparisons are not included here, but elsewhere in this book I lean on the work of Robert Coles (1971) and on the suggestive laboratory experiments of performance in biracial groups of Irwin Katz (1967) and Elizabeth Cohen et al. (1970). I have also ruled out one-celled studies in which no comparison is involved, studies in which the only comparison is between black and white children, and studies in which the races are not analyzed separately. Finally, I have omitted any study reported with insufficient detail to allow categorization or the findings of which are unclear to me.

The review that follows summarizes the research of interest under the general headings of anxiety, self-concept, and aspiration, three of the most frequently studied psychological outcomes of school desegregation.

2. ANXIETY

"When I talk about school, my mother think I am happy But most of the time am sad" (black girl in desegregated sixth-grade classroom)

"If I could change myself I would like to become a goste and scar all the people that beat me exsept

my mother or any other relative" (black boy in desegregated sixth-grade classroom)

"If I could change myself I wod be a big big big dog and kill evebohy."(white boy in a sixth-grade classroom, the only white child in a black school)

As indicated previously, the greatest concern of psychologists contemplating the onset of desegregation was over the emotional stress they feared for transferred black children. In fact, there has been little clear evidence of serious effects in this regard.

It is true that in the Deep South black children who transfer to previously all-white schools face extreme rejection. A survey of such children in Alabama revealed that 25% went expecting physical injury or harm and 63% expected white students to be smarter than they (Chesler and Segal, 1967). But Coles (1967), who studied southern black pioneers in school desegregation under extremely stressful circumstances, says he found, together with symptoms of fear and anxiety (loss of appetite, nightmares, lethargy), extraordinary resiliency and light-heartedness through suffering. Moreover, his observations (1968) of northern desegregation by busing convinced him that the children he studied came to no notable psychiatric harm.

Chart A-5 summarizes seven studies that report the relation of school desegregation to measured anxiety. It is apparent that the predictions of psychologists do not receive strong support from these data. A typical finding, reported by researchers in both Ann Arbor (Carrigan, 1969) and Hartford (Mahan, 1968), is that the general anxiety level of black children is higher than that of white children, but there is no increase in measured anxiety following transfer to a racially mixed school. On the other hand, one study of desegregation by pairing in new York City discovered that black pupils showed higher levels of anxiety on the Sarason Scale in the paired schools than in the segregated school, a difference significant at the .06 level (Slone, 1968). Similarly, black boys placed in suburban or independent secondary schools by Project ABC showed increases over two years on all anxiety-related measures, in comparison with a control group who remained in ghetto schools (Wessman, 1969).

It is probable that many children are more worried than tests reveal and that hidden anxiety may be a factor in slow response to the stimulus of desegregated schools.[14] If there is "recursive feedback" between attitudes and performance, as suggested by the work of Katz (1967), children who fear failure therefore achieve below capacity and thus become all the more fearful. Further research on the relation between anxiety and achievement in biracial classrooms is overdue.

3. SELF-CONFIDENCE

"If I could change myself, I would change my nationality maybe." (black boy, grade 6)

"If I could change myself I would think of myself as being smart" (black girl, grade 6)

"If I could change myself I would not want to change my self because I like my self the way I am." (black boy, grade 6)

It has frequently been assumed by psychologists of both races that the self-esteem of black children tends to be low. By internalizing white racist attitudes the children supposedly develop individual and group self-hatred, sense of inadequacy, low self-esteem. Segregation, as a symbol of their inferior status, is considered especially damaging. And, this theory continues, desegregation should undo some of the harm and raise self-esteem.

But a recent study of the self-esteem of black youth by Rosenberg and Simmons (1971) throws doubt on the assumption that blacks have lower self-esteem than whites and on the assumption that black self-esteem is lower in segregated than in desegregated schools. These authors interviewed 1917 third- to twelfth-grade pupils in 26 Baltimore schools and used a validated scale measuring how highly the subject regarded himself *in general*.[15] They found that the blacks in their sample appeared to have higher, not lower, self-esteem than whites. They then reviewed 12 other studies of race and self-esteem and concluded that "a reasonably conservative assessment would be that there are no appreciable racial differences in self-esteem; this too is the fundamental conclusion we draw from our own study" (p. 8).

Rosenberg and Simmons also investigated the effect of racial insulation on self-esteem, confining their attention to secondary schools for lack of sufficient cases at the elementary level. At the junior high level the self-esteem differences between majority-white and majority-black schools were "modest," but at the senior high level the difference was statistically significant: 12% of black children in predominantly black schools, but 26% of black children in predominantly white schools showed low self-esteem.

Similar findings are reported by other researchers who have studied the effect of school racial mixture on black self-esteem. Either no significant relationship between these variables is found, or the relation is negative, though sometimes the findings vary with the sex, age, or other status of the subject. As the review that follows indicates, a strong positive relation between black self-concept and school percentage white is rarely reported.

Forty studies of desegregation and the self-attitudes of black children are summarized in Chart A-6. All except one were conducted between 1966 and 1971. Six use national or regional samples; the rest are based on (mostly small) local samples scattered across the nation. Half of the subjects are in secondary school, the rest in elementary school.

The most common criterion variable in this group of studies is general self-esteem, sometimes called self-image, self-concept, or personal self, but usually with an evaluative connotation. Several studies separate academic self-concept from general self-concept and examine the effect of desegregation on one or both of these constructs. Items to measure sense of control of the environment were included in the EEOS survey and have been borrowed by several subsequent investigations.[16] In addition, there are two or three investigations of hard-to-categorize traits such as self-acceptance, self-other relations, and adjustment.

The instruments used to measure these qualities present more of a problem than their definitions, being almost as numerous as the studies. Included are nonverbal self-portraits and picture sorts, sentence completion or semiprojective instruments, semantic differentials, questionnaires, as well as more standardized tests and scales. In comparison with achievement tests, tests of self-concept are not only less highly standardized but also seem to be less frequently validated for use on a minority group population.[17] The study by Rosenberg and Simmons mentioned earlier is unusual in the attention paid to scale validation. Comparing black and white children, the authors find identical internal reliability of items and similar association between scale results and theoretically derived variables; that is, they find strong evidence of construct validity.

The most common design of the studies is a cross-sectional comparison of segregated and desegregated subjects without any measure of change or growth. In many cases there is no attempt to match subjects on social class or other background variables. In other words, any personality differences between the groups could have many causes other than school percentage white. Most of the longitudinal or four-celled studies are also without controls on other variables, though this lack is less serious when subjects are tested before and after desegregation.

As a way of summarizing the findings of studies of desegregation and self-concept, Chart 3-1 presents a frequency distribution according to dimension of self-concept and the direction and statistical significance of any relation with school percentage white.

Chart 3-1. *Frequency Distribution of Empirical Studies of Relation of School Desegregation and Self-Concept of Black Students*

	General Self-Esteem				Academic Self-Esteem				Sense of Environmental Control			
Direction of Difference	+	–	0	Mixed	+	–	0	Mixed	+	–	0	Mixed
Significant differences	4	3	7	5	1	1	1	2	2			4
No significant differences but trends		5				2			1			
No significance tests		1				2	1					
Total studies	4	9	7	5	1	5	2	2	3			4

Studies which measure more than one dimension of self-concept are counted more than once.

Of 25 studies that measure *general self-esteem*,[18] 9 find that desegregation shows negative effect (but in only 3 of these is the difference statistically significant), 7 no effect, 5 mixed effect, and 4 positive effect. The studies that find a significant negative effect are all cross-sectional. Of these researchers, only Rosenberg and Simmons give careful attention to the possibility of spuriousness. Of the four studies that find a positive effect the only one with adequate sample and design is the most recent evaluation of the ABC scholarship program mentioned above, which places highly selected students in independent schools (Perry, 1973). The report shows a significant two-year rise in the self-esteem of a matched control group. This last finding aside, there is little support for the assumption that desegregation of public schools automatically raises black self-esteem.

The mixed findings in regard to the relation of school percentage white to self-esteem are very suggestive as to the probable preconditions of successful desegregation. For instance, male self-image benefits from desegregation and female self-image does not, according to two researchers (Denmark, 1970; Powell and Fuller, 1970). In Miami, Florida, it was necessary to specify the family background of subjects, since in the first year of desegregation differences were in favor of the integrated setting for the middle-class children only, whereas in the second year they were in favor of lower-class children (Walker, 1968). If, as these findings suggest, girls and lower-class children are more vulnerable to the stresses of desegregation, they require more staff support in racially mixed schools. Desegregated faculties are also apparently advisable. Another investigator compared black self-concept in newly desegregated schools, in segregated schools with desegrated faculty, and in segregated schools with segregated faculty. In integrated schools subjects gained only on "physical self," not on other dimensions of self-concept. Total score was highest in black schools with at least one white teacher (Williams and Byars, 1970).

The circumstances surrounding desegregation apparently also affect the outcome. One psychologist found to her surprise that children in a peacefully integrated school showed lower self-esteem than children in either a segregated school or in a school desegregated under anxiety-arousing circumstances, and she speculates that high self-esteem in the latter school might reflect high morale in the tightly knit Negro community following a successful desegregation battle (Meketon, 1966). Another mixed finding is that reported in the earlier evaluation of Project ABC: "ABC boys became more tense and less driven, yet paradoxically more self-assured and independent."[19]

Academic self-concept is usually measured by an item that asks pupils to estimate their own ability in relation to class-mates. When desegregation involves crossing social class as well as racial lines, the norm against which pupils evaluate themselves may well be higher. It is not surprising therefore that, as Chart 3-1 shows, academic self-concept tends to fall with school percentage white.[20] However, in the study of Boston sixth graders I found that academic self-concept was negatively related to present school percentage white but positively related to past school percentage white, suggesting that the long-run benefits of a more challenging academic environment may be greater than the short-run discouragement involved (St. John, 1971).

A much publicized finding of the Coleman Report (1966) was that (for the large sample of children surveyed) academic self-concept fell but *sense of environmental control* rose with school percentage white. No controls on social class or other variables were applied in these analyses. But when the U.S. Commission on Civil Rights (1967a), controlling on individual and peer SES, examined the relation of percentage white in last year's classroom to student's responses on the items of Cole-man's control scale, a positive effect for classroom integration was found for ninth- and twelfth-grade students in northeastern cities. Similarly, McPartland's (1968) reanalysis of these data indicated that early school desegregation as well as classroom percentage white contributed significantly and positively to sense of control, even with SES held constant. "Of all the attitude items, the desegregation effects are strongest and most constant for this measure of sense of opportunity and control of environment" (p. 208).

Another national cross-sectional study which tested these variables was Bachman's (1970) study of tenth-grade boys in 87 high schools. No difference in self-concept or sense of control was found between white and black boys in northern integrated, northern segregated, or southern segregated high schools. However, when family background and IQ were controlled, the more segregated the environment, the higher was self-esteem (either general or academic).

To summarize, the evidence of these studies considered as a group is that the effect of school desegregation on the general or academic self-concept of minority group members tends to be negative or mixed more often than positive. Moreover, in the most careful study of the topic, Rosenberg and Simmons found that self-esteem was significantly lower in desegregated schools. On the other hand, sense of control is found to be either positively related or unrelated to school percentage white, but it is never negatively related.[21] Even this conclusion, however, must remain tentative in view of the fact that none of these studies combined an experimental design, the matching of control and experimental groups on all relevant variables, and the use of scales validated on a black population.

In this connection, five studies of the self-attitudes of segregated and desegregated adults suggest not only the long-term benefits of desegregation but also the selection bias parents probably introduce into studies of the effects of school desegregation on their children. Thus, comparing 30 residentially desegregated and 30 matched segregated black households in Detroit, Haggstrom (1962) found higher self-esteem for the former. Bullough (1969) reported that a sample of middle-class suburban blacks showed less alienation, powerlessness, and anomie than middle-class ghetto residents. Both Haggstrom's and Bullough's respondents achieved integration through their own efforts and had found the experience satisfying. Works (1962) compared black residents of the integrated and segregated sections of a low-income housing project. Integrated respondents reported more improvement than segregated respondents in self-concept measured by a 20-item semantic differential scale. Crain (1971), in a survey of 1600 adult blacks in northern metropolitan areas, found that those who had attended integrated schools were more likely to live in integrated neighborhoods, to indicate a sense of control over their environment, and to call themselves happy.[22]

Thus in the long run desegregation is usually found associated with higher self-esteem. But the short-run outcome tends to be lower self-esteem, though this depends on many individual and situational factors.

Most studies of school race and self-concept have ignored the classroom process and its contribution to psychological health. Some investigators have questioned parents and teachers and generally find their attitudes to be favorable. But objective data on school interracial climate are rare. However, Rosenberg and Simmons do inquire into the mechanisms by which desegregation may lower the self-esteem of minority group members and show evidence that the desegreated children in their sample were thereby exposed to racial prejudice, to cultural dissonance, and to stiff academic competition. As I will suggest in Chapter 5, these mechanisms are probably generally applicable.

4. ASPIRATION

"Someday I will Grow up and be a teach cause I Like school." (black boy, grade 6)

"Someday I will go to Radcliffe College and become a singer." (black girl, grade 6)

"When I look in the mirror I see some greatness" (black boy, grade 9)

Social science findings on the aspirations of black youth challenge the same assumptions as do findings on self-concept. Hopes and plans for the future prove to be as high for blacks as for whites and to be higher in predominantly black schools than in predominantly white schools.

Of the 25 studies of desegregation and aspirations listed in Chart A-7, all except four have high school students as subjects. The preferences of younger children are usually assumed to show considerable admixture of fantasy and to bear slight relation to eventual course of action. However, even high school seniors may dream. Researchers thus usually use questionnaire items that distinguish between hopes (or preferences) and plans (or expectations). Aspirations are further categorized according to whether they refer to desired education or occupation. Occupational aspiration is a dependent variable in over half of these studies, and in all cases except one the questionnaire item refers to occupational "preference" or "choice" rather than "plan." In the studies of educational aspirations, however, plans are solicited more often than preferences, though the studies which ask students for both plans and preferences find that the two are similarly related (or *not* related) to school percentage white.

In contrast to studies that depend on oral responses through questionnaires or interviews, some researchers use behavioral measures of motivation or aspiration, such as absenteeism, dropout rate, or the pupil's selection from among tasks graded according to difficulty. One important but little studied outcome of school desegregation is rate of college attendance. Only one research report was found that included this variable.

The design was cross-sectional for the great majority of studies of the effect of desegregation on aspiration (17 out of 24). Moreover, control on family background was probably inadequate in most cases. A notable exception on both counts is the study by Perry (1973) of the effect of participation in the ABC program on ghetto youth placed in independent schools. Perry matched 47 ABC youths with 47 non-ABC youths (on community size, father presence, parental education and income, previous GPA and test scores) and compared changes from sophomore to senior year in the aspirations of the two groups. For both groups aspirations rose, so that participation in the program made no significant difference in measured change in questionnaire response. However, 94% of the ABC students, in comparison with 62% of non-ABC's, thereafter entered college, and the colleges they entered were more selective than those entered by non-ABC's.

Of three other four-celled studies,[23] one reported a negative relation and one a positive relation between aspirations and school precentage white. However, Armor's findings of a significant decline in college plans for METCO students bused to Boston suburbs relative to their METCO siblings is thrown into question when we consider that the control group of siblings was small, nonrandom, unmatched, and tested under different conditions from the experimental group.[24]

Three cross-sectional studies with national samples are included in Chart A-6. Armor (1967) used the EEOS data to analyze the college plans of Negro youth by school percentage white. The relation was positive only for upper ability ninth-grade males in the northeast. For all other groups (girls, twelfth graders, and lower ability students), plans were highest in segregated schools.[25] Bachman (1970), studying a nationwide sample of tenth-grade boys, found that educational aspirations of segregated blacks in the South were higher than those of segregated northerners, which in turn were higher than those of integrated northerners. On the other hand, Lindsay and Gottlieb (1969) used a NORC nationwide sample to study the aspirations and expectations of male twelfth-grade students in 55 metropolitan high schools. They report an increase in aspirations and expectations as school percentage white increases. Since these researchers and Armor were both using national metropolitan samples surveyed in the mid-1960s it is hard to understand why their findings should conflict, as they do in regard to twelfth-grade males. The most probable explanation is inadequate control on family background by Lindsay and Gottlieb. Students in integrated high schools probably tend to come from homes that encourage high aspirations.

In my studies of desegregation in two northern cities, I compared the black graduates of segregated and integrated elementary schools in regard to the aspirations they expressed when in high school. In New Haven I found that the educational and occupational plans and preferences of all 230 black eleventh graders were unrelated to the racial composition of their elementary schools, even with birthplace (North or South) and family SES held constant. But the trend was for aspirations to be highest for the graduates of majority black elementary schools (St. John, 1966). In Pittsburgh I found statistically significant differences by school percentage white in the educational aspirations of a sample of 1388 ninth graders (two-thirds of the blacks at that grade level in the city). And again aspirations were highest for the graduates of black elementary schools (St. John, 1973).

Chart 3-2 summarizes the findings on aspiration in the same manner that findings on self-concept were summarized. It is evident that significant positive findings are rare. For both

Chart 3-2. Frequency Distribution of Empirical Studies of Relation of School Desegregation and Aspiration of Black Students

Direction of Difference	Educational Aspiration				Occupational Aspiration			
	+	−	0	Mixed	+	−	0	Mixed
Significant difference		5	4		1	1	3	1
No significant difference but trends		2		1		3		
No significance tests but trends	1	2		1	2	1		1
Total studies	1	9	4	2	3	5	3	2

educational and occupational aspirations, the relation with school percentage white tends to be negative.

5. "THE ANSWERS ARE NOT ALL IN"

Jencks writes, "Unfortunately, the methodology of attitude research is not sufficiently well developed for us to separate the effects of initial traits from the effects of schooling. In the absence of evidence, we are inclined to believe that the relationship between schooling and noncognitive traits is much like the relationship between schooling and cognitive traits" (Jencks et al., 1972c, p. 134). In other words this relationship too is due primarily to selection.

The studies reviewed in this chapter are not immune to this criticism. Rarely does the design allow for matching of experimental and control group before the onset of desegregation. Rarely can we be sure that differences that appear later between the segregated and the desegregated were not there to start with. However, given the general direction of findings, it is unlikely that selection has been an important factor. Both the self-concept and aspiration of black children tend to be stronger in segregated schools, whereas one would expect the self-confident and the ambitious to choose racially mixed schools. It seems as though desegregation must be dysfunctional in some ways for minority youth.

One issue that has not been resolved is whether "realism" is an important dimension of aspiration and self-concept. Are these attitudes functional only if they are in line with the abilities of individuals and with opportunities in the social structure? If ability is high but aspiration low, the obvious solution to the dissonance appears to be raising aspiration. But in the opposite case of high aspiration and low evidence of ability, the recourse is probably not to trim aspiration (though some observers, including Cicourel and Kitsuse, 1963, have suggested that this is the automatic policy of many school counselors). Measures of ability may be inaccurate, so that scores and grades do injustice to the academic potential of culturally deprived students (Fishman et al., 1964). Moreover, the verbalization of high aspiration and self-confidence does not prove that these attitudes are sufficiently internalized to affect behavior. Finally, as opportunities for higher education and jobs are opened to poor youth with modest credentials, high aspirations on their part may not be at all unrealistic.

Atkinson's (1964) theory of achievement risk behavior is that choice of a very easy or very difficult course of action indicates low aspiration. Katz (1967), too, has argued that lower and more realistic aspiration has more motive power for black youth than defensive overaspiration. Thus Veroff and Peele (1969) interpret a reduction in aspiration on a laboratory task on the part of desegregated black grade-school boys in a midwestern community as evidence of positive gain. If we adopt this line of reasoning, we will no longer consider findings from New Haven, Pittsburgh, the EEOS, or Bachman that lower aspirations for the desegregated lend support to school segregation. Instead they suggest that desegregated youth may be more ready to take moderate risks in pursuit of realistic ambitions.

"Among the potentials of social research," wrote Elizabeth Herzog (1970), "is its ability to contribute to the making or breaking of social stereotypes" (p. 10). "We cannot afford to wait until all the answers are in. But neither can we afford to publicize prematurely answers based on fragmentary findings inadequately analyzed—answers that in effect we do not really have" (p. 122). In my view, the psychological "benefits"—or "hazards"—of school desegregation are such stereotypes as long as they remain undifferentiated. As I will suggest in Chapter 6, we must ask: Benefits or hazards in what respects? For what types of children? Under what circumstances? Social scientists, having contributed to the making of these stereotypes, now have the responsibility to break them through more adequate analysis of less fragmentary findings.

NOTES

1. A. Lee Coleman (1960) summarized social science predictions about desegregation, 1950-1955. Predictions in this period, says Coleman, related "to short-range results or the concomitants of change and change efforts, and would thus be classified under process, rather than long-range outcomes" (p. 260).

2. See Van den Haag (1960) or Garrett (1966).

3. For instance, Arendt (1959), Armstrong and Gregor (1964), or Bronfen-brenner (1967).

4. For further discussion of the predictions of social scientists, see Weinberg (1970).

5. For example, see *U.S. News and World Report* (1956); Pettigrew (1964); "Replies to Jensen", *Harvard Educational Review* (1969).

6. For example, Milner (1953); Holland (1964); Coles (1967).

7. Bernard (1958); Ausubel and Ausubel (1963); Haggstrom (1962).

8. Pinderhughes (1964).

9. Clark (1965).

10. See also Wolf (1972).

11. See Feldman (1971) for a helpful discussion of the benefits and hazards of such integrative studies.

12. One quarter of the studies reported below are dissertations. All of these have been read, for the most part on microfilm.

13. The most helpful sources have been Weinberg (1970), Zirkel (1971), *Psychological Abstracts, Dissertation Abstracts,* ERIC, *Educational Index,* and the indices of educational and psychological journals, as well as the writings of psychologists such as Pettigrew (1964, 1967, 1969) and Katz (1967).

14. In Riverside, Gerard and Miller (1971) find significantly higher test anxiety as well as general anxiety for Mexican-Americans and blacks than for majority group children, but show other evidence that leads them to question whether the lower achievement of minority group children can be attributed to their level of anxiety.

15. A random sample of 2625 pupils was drawn and 78% of these were interviewed, in most cases by a person of the same race. Moreover, no evidence of bias was found in cases where subject and interviewer were not of the same race.

16. Coleman (1966). Agree or Disagree:

Good luck is more important than hard work for success.

Every time I try to get ahead, something or someone stops me.

People like me don't have much of a chance to be successful in life.

17. See Fishman et al. (1964) for further discussion of this problem.

18. Included here are the following studies which measure "general self-esteem," "general self-concept," "self-perception," "self-image," "satisfaction with self," "evaluative rating of self," and "racial self-esteem": Aberdeen (1969), Bachman (1970), Barber (1968), Bienvenu (1968), Carrigan (1969), Denmark (1970), Garth (1969), Griffin (1969), Harootunian (1968), Jessup (1967), Knight (1970), Lockwood (1966), McPartland (1968), McWhirt (1967), Meketon (1966), Perry (1973), Powell and Fuller (1970), Rosenberg and Simmons (1971), St. John (1969, 1971), Scott (1969), Taylor (1967), Walker (1968), D.E. Williams (1968), R.L. Williams and Byars (1970), Zirkel and Moses (1971).

19. Wessman (1969) found that on the Cattell HSPG, ABC students showed a significant increase in overall anxiety with no significant changes for the matched non-ABC controls. On the Gough CPI, the ABC students showed a significant increase in self-acceptance and social presence and a slight increase in sense of well-being, but a significant decrease in socialization. This test was not administered to the control group.

20. The ten studies of desegregation and academic self-concept are Armor (1972b), Bachman (1970), Coleman (1966), Gardner (1970), Hsia (1971), Lammers (1969), Moorefield (1967), St. John (1971), Strauss (1967), and Walker (1968).

21. The seven studies of desegregation and sense of control are: Bachman (1970), Coleman (1966), McPartland (1968), Perry (1973), St. John (1969, 1971), U.S. Commission (1967a).

22. Residence in stable integrated or segregated neighborhoods is quite different from residence in racially changing neighborhoods. Thus the above findings are not contradicted by a recent study by Wilson (1971), in which anomie was found to be higher in a transitional zone (63% black) than in a neighborhood that was 96% black. Wilson's finding does suggest, however, that one explanation for contradictory findings as to the relation between desegregation and self-attitudes may be lack of comparability across studies in the definition of the independent variable.

23. Armor (1972a); Falk, Cosby, and Wright (1973); and McWhirt (1967).

24. For further discussion of the methodoligical weaknesses of this study, see Pettigrew et al. (1973).

25. Jencks et al. (1972c) report on another reanalysis of the EEOS data on twelfth grade aspirations: "When we compared individuals with similar family background and test scores, those in predominantly black schools had the same aspirations as those in predominantly white schools" (p. 154).

"What seems to me really unfair is the way some Negro's are treated in an all white school" (black girl, grade 9)

"What seems to me really unfair is how coloreds push whites around" (white girl, grade 9)

'The best thing about this school are the Jewish kids they are very friendly people" (black boy, grade 9)

"The worst thing about this school is the colored kids think your always against them" (white boy, grade 9)

"I wish this school like[d] me to go [to it], and I wish this school's people like me." (Chinese-American boy, grade 6)

4. Desegregation and Racial Prejudice [1]

1. MEASURING PREJUDICE

Among the goals of school desegregation programs, the reduction of majority group prejudice is cited almost as frequently as the promotion of minority group achievement and self-confidence. If, as Myrdal (1944) argued, segregation is a key factor in maintaining the vicious circle of discrimination, inferiority, and the reinforcement of prejudice, then desegregation should open the way for equality of opportunity and of attainment and thus for the elimination of prejudice on the part of both races. Is this in fact the usual outcome?

Children do not enter first grade devoid of racial prejudice. A considerable body of research over the past two decades has shown that awareness of racial differences develops by the age of three or four and that positive or negative feelings toward these differences follow soon thereafter.[2] Parents are assumed by many researchers[3] to be the primary source of racial attitudes in children. Indeed a number of researchers have found moderate but statistically significant positive correlations between the scores of children on scales measuring prejudice and the attitudes of their own parents.[4]

As children grow older the influence of the home presumably lessens and that of school and peers presumably grows, but there has been little definitive study of the relative contribution of parents, teachers, and peers to the development of intergroup attitudes. The scholars whose works are reviewed in this chapter assume that school-aged children are racially prejudiced. They have sought to determine whether only one aspect of childrens' lives — their school's black/white ratio — affects their level of prejudice.

Psychologists distinguish between three components of intergroup attitudes, the cognitive, affective, and conative. The cognitive component includes racial awareness, beliefs about racial differences, and ideology concerning appropriate race relations. The affective component includes positive and negative feelings toward the other group and toward interracial association. The conative component, or action set, involves predispositions to behave in certain ways. Finally there is action or behavior itself, which may or may not adhere closely to beliefs, feelings, or action set.

Investigation of the effects of desegregation on interracial acceptance faces a methodological problem not present when the spotlight is on achievement or personality: interracial *behavior* cannot be compared in segregated and integrated settings or before and after desegregation; it can be examined only if the races are in contact. Thus three types of studies of interracial acceptance among school children are available: (1) comparison of interracial attitudes, beliefs, or social distance, not behavior, in segregated and desegregated schools (either cross-sectional or before-and-after); (2) studies of interracial friendship choice or behavior in desegregated settings only, which attempt to relate such behavior to previous interracial contact or to racial percentages in the classroom, or to measure changes in behavior over time in the desegregated situations; and (3) case studies of acceptance or cleavage in desegregated schools or classrooms. Studies of the first two types provide some evidence of the effects of school racial composition; studies of the third type, although revealing about the potentials of desegregation, cannot properly measure its effect, since no comparison is involved.

Researchers of the first type, who compare racial attitudes in segregated and desegregated settings, use a wide variety of instruments — questionnaires, social distance scales, adjective checklists, semantic differentials, and doll play — but often pay scant attention to the reliability or validity of the tests they employ. Usually the test is presumed to have face validity and its items to have the same meaning for black and white children, though these may be questionable assumptions. The correlation between results of different tests administered to the same subjects is rarely reported, though it is not clear what such coefficients (if available) would prove. Less than perfect correlation is to be expected between the cognitive, affective, and conative components of prejudice. (Ehrlich, 1973, p. 106).

Sociometry, as compared with scales that tap the cognitive and affective components of prejudice, attempts to measure behavior, or at least behavioral predisposition. As developed by Moreno (1934) and described by Lindzey and Borgotta, sociometry "involves each member of the group privately specifying a number of other persons in the group with whom he wishes to engage in some particular activity" (1954, p. 407). School researchers often modify Moreno's procedure by asking a student to name his friends or to rate his classmates. Such techniques have been used over the last 30 years to assess the racial preferences of school children, and the findings are in one respect quite stable: ethnic own-group preference appears to be a universal phenomenon. But it is not clear whether such preference indicates positive self-concept and ethnic identification or rejection of and hostility to the other group. In view of the well-documented historical tendency of blacks to engage in self-rejection, there seems to be good reason for interpreting any increase in own-group preference on their part as a positive gain in self-esteem. But increased own-group preference on the part of white children, who typically suffer from a sense of racial superiority, might well be an indication of increased prejudice. Studies which do not structure the choice between own group and other group in a zero-sum fashion show that growth in friendliness to both races often proceeds simultaneously (Paige, 1970).

2.   COMPARATIVE STUDIES[5]

As in previous chapters, I have charted the available research on the topic before us, the effect of school racial composition on attitudes and behavior toward the other race. The 41 studies listed in Charts A-8 and A-9 span the years 1937–1973 but are clustered in the late 1960s. The great majority were conducted in the North. Samples range in size from under 100 to over 3000. The grade level is secondary somewhat more often than elementary, with a few studies involving preschool children. Some investigators, considering prejudice a white problem, focus on the effect of desegregation on white students only. But more often intergroup relations is viewed as a two-way process and the outcomes for blacks as well as whites are examined.

The reader of these studies does not easily get a clear picture of the direction of their findings. A glance at Charts A-8 and A-9 shows that for either race positive findings are less common than negative findings and that in as many cases there is no effect or mixed effects. It is also apparent that the direction of findings is as often contradictory as it is consistent for the two races. Sometimes desegregation is reported to have ameliorated the prejudice of whites but intensified that of blacks, sometimes the reverse.

Racial Attitudes.   Brief mention of one or two of the most carefully executed studies at each level will point up the diversity of findings.

At the *preschool* level, Porter (1971) used choice of brown or white dolls as indication of the racial attitudes of three- and four-year-olds in Boston nursery schools. Attendance at an interracial school was associated with higher racial awareness on the part of both races and with preference for dolls of the other race among white boys (not girls) and among light-skinned (not dark-skinned) Negro children.

In the schools studied by Porter, the staffs apparently did not openly promote race awareness and acceptance. In fact, Porter did not consider that the majority of schools she studied were "adequately integrated," since race was ignored as an issue of importance. In contrast, Crooks (1970) compared children without any preschool experience and those who had spent a year in a racially balanced school with teachers "who deliberately emphasized racial differences and discussed those differences in favorable terms." Both black and white children who had been in the program showed more acceptance of brown dolls than those who had not. But, as suggested above, it is not clear whether this outcome for black children should be considered evidence of positive self-concept or a negative racial attitude.

At the *elementary school level* Dentler and Elkins (1967) found that in the New York schools they studied the prejudice of white children increased with the percentage black of the school. On the other hand, in one of the most careful studies of children at this age, Singer (1966) reported that black and white fifth graders in an integrated New York school used fewer critical stereotypes and were ready to associate more closely with the other racial group than children matched on IQ and SES in segregated schools. Another researcher, comparing fourth and fifth graders in "white-dominated" (undefined) and "mixed" schools in Sacramento, California, found that white, black, and Japanese-Americans assigned negative traits to the other racial groups significantly more often in the "white-dominated" school (Kurokawa, 1971).

Junior high school integration may be particularly difficult to achieve, since children tend to be especially ingroup during early adolescence. It is no surprise, therefore, that two studies at this grade level report that racial mixing has negative effects. Webster (1961) found that after six months together in a California school, white pupils were significantly more prejudiced and became significantly less accepting of blacks than white control subjects in a segregated school. At the same time, however, black pupils became significantly more accepting of whites. In upstate New York, eighth-grade pupils in an open enrollment school, in a suburban white school, and in a black ghetto school were questioned as to their racial attitudes. Both blacks and whites showed more prejudice in the open enrollment schools, a reflection, according to the researcher, of the very hostile attitude to the program on the part of the local white community (Barber, 1968). On the other hand, in a voluntary busing program for parochial school pupils in Chicago, it was found that the desegregated of both races had more favorable views of each other than did the segregated (Gardner et al., 1970).

At the *high school level* the reports of several studies of southern samples indicate that mixed schooling led either to no change or to deterioration in the interracial attitudes of white students but to an improvement in the attitudes of black students. Thus Lombardi (1962) reported no significant change in the attitudes of whites in the year following desegregation of a

Maryland high school, and Campbell (1956) found that in the six months after desegregation in Oak Ridge, Tennessee, white students changed in a negative more often than in a positive direction. McWhirt (1967) in South Carolina compared tenth graders in three high schools, one white, one black, and one desegragated. White students were more negative and black students were less negative to the other group in the desegregated school.

Two studies of high school students in the northeast found that previous interracial contact was associated with favorable interracial attitudes on the part of whites, McPartland's (1968) reanalysis of the USOE survey data and Useem's (1971) analysis of white students' reactions to a program that bused urban blacks into Boston area suburban schools (METCO). But although the attitudes of white students in METCO schools were generally favorable, the bused black students reported decreasing interaction with them and showed a significant increase in separatist ideology in the course of a year (Armor, 1972).[6]

Sociometric Choosing.   The effect of classroom or school racial composition on sociometric choosing is hard to pinpoint. Most investigators find, as McParland (1968) did for his Equality of Educational Opportunity (EEOS) sample, that "as the proportion of students from the other race increases in a student's classes, the proportion of those who have close friends outside of their own race increases" (p. 236). But if friendships were racially random the same effect would be observed. The use of an index which corrects for racial percentages and therefore for the probability of ingroup or outgroup choice[7] usually reveals the opposite tendency; students become more ingroup in their friendships as they become more racially isolated.

Another way of studying the effect of contact on interracial friendship is to relate current sociometric choice to past exposure. Thus I found that in Pittsburgh the number of choices black ninth graders received from and gave to whites was significantly related to their average school percentage white in earlier years (St. John, 1969).

Finally, there are studies which compare interracial friendship choices before and after a period of time in a desegregated situation. Yarrow, Campbell, and Yarrow (1958) reported that after two weeks of interracial camp children of both races "still tend to prefer white cabin mates as friends, but there is a statistically significant drop in the extent to which they are the favored group" (p. 22).

3. THE SEARCH FOR CONDITIONING FACTORS

The studies discussed in the previous section are not a random sample but were selected to indicate that findings are inconsistent and mixed. In the hope of discovering variables that would account for seeming anomalies across all 41 studies, I have asked a series of questions of the data.

1. Is the direction of the findings similar for studies of attitudes and studies of sociometric choosing?

A tally of the direction of findings by type of study is one way of comparing the effect of desegregation on attitudes and behavior. It should be stressed, however, that no 'statistical significance is claimed for this tally or for those on subsequent pages which classify studies according to other characteristics. The tally reflects the nonrandom locations, dates, and circumstances of desegregation experiments and studies thereof. Moreover, I have omitted studies on which information is lacking for a particular count and counted a study twice if two tests of the hypothesis were involved. In some cases I count as positive certain findings that the researcher considered negative. For instance, though I recognize that a gain in self-concept may be involved, more frequent choice of brown dolls by desegregated black children is here considered a negative finding. Finally, the decision to count findings as mixed or as positive or negative is somewhat arbitrary. For instance, there is often a significant overall trend, but there may also be significantly different findings for members of subgroups (i.e., boys and girls). If the difference is pronounced I call the findings mixed.

With this reservation in mind, let us look at the direction of findings for the 23 studies of racial attitudes, social-distance, or stereotyping and for the 17 studies of sociometric choosing listed in Chart A-8.

Direction of Findings		Attitude Studies	Sociometric Studies
Whites	+	8	3
	–	8	3
	0	1	6
	Mixed	2	4
Blacks	+	5	1
	–	6	4
	0	1	5
	Mixed	2	4

For white children the type of instrument apparently makes no difference in whether positive or negative findings are reported.

For black children there is a greater tendency for the findings to be negative when the instrument is a sociometric test. It is also apparent that for both races the most usual finding of sociometric studies is No Difference.

Whether sociometric or observed behavior in the classroom corresponds with expressed attitudes toward the other race has been virtually ignored in desegregation research. Porter (1971) found no positive correlation for either race between doll preference and observed playmate choice. In fact, in one school the relationship was negative, leading Porter to conclude that (even for five-year-olds with intense racial attitudes) sex, personality, and play style are more salient determinants of friendship than race (p. 168). The same lack of consistency between general attitudes and behavior toward specific individuals of the other race may prevail among older children as well.

2. Does the design of the study affect the findings? Do longitudinal studies show statistically significant differences more often than cross-sectional studies?

The design is cross-sectional in two studies out of three, involving either a comparison of segregated and recently desegregated pupils or else a search for correlation between degree of prejudice and school racial composition. Proper longitudinal studies which measure change over time are rare; researchers more frequently try to relate present attitude to past racial contact. Only nine studies gathered change measures for pupils in balanced as well as inbalanced schools. In all except one of these studies the time between tests was less than a year. In other words, the long-term effect of desegregation on interracial attitudes and behavior has hardly been measured at all.

Examination of direction of findings by study design indicates that for white children cross-sectional studies without before and after measurement suggest attitudinal gains, but four-celled studies show attitudinal losses. No clear correlation between design and findings is suggested for black children.

3. Does self-selection of desegregated schools by the unprejudiced explain the relationship between school racial composition and racial attitudes?

Design

Direction of Findings		Cross-Sectional	Longitudinal	Four-Celled
Whites	+	10	1	0
	−	5		6
	0	4	2	1
	Mixed	5		1
Blacks	+	5		2
	−	6	1	3
	0	4	2	
	Mixed	6		

Adequate control of other variables is lacking in many studies. For instance, we are often not told whether the effect of desegregation varied with the sex, achievement level, or social class background of subjects, though others have found that these variables interact with school racial composition in their effect on interracial attitudes. The factor that is most likely to contaminate research on this topic is the self-selection of the desegregated situation by those with the most favorable attitudes. It is therefore important to note how desegregation came about.

In over a third of these studies racially mixed schools resulted from neighborhood housing patterns. It is likely that many black families in these neighborhoods had attitudes favorable to desegregation and to whites. White children in these schools are more likely to come from households that had lived in the neighborhood before blacks moved in. Their predispositions toward desegregation might well be unfavorable.

In another third of the studies black pupils were enrolled in racially mixed schools through open enrollment or a voluntary busing program. In this situation, too, black parents and children could be presumed to be pro-integration, whereas no such presumption can be made as to receiving-school parents and children.

It is only in cases of involuntary desegregation mandated by court or school board that the self-selection factor can be ruled out for both racial groups. And among the communities where the effect of desegregation on racial attitudes has been studied, mandatory desegregation has to date been rare.

How Desegregation Came About

Direction of Findings		Neighbor- hood	Voluntary (pre-school, open enroll- ment, or volunteer for busing program)	Mandatory (school board deci- sion, or re- ceive open enrollment pupils)	Not Speci- fied
Whites	+	4	3	3	1
	−	5	0	6	0
	0	2	1	3	1
	Mixed	3	1	2	0
Blacks	+	1	3	1	2
	−	3	5	2	0
	0	4	1	0	1
	Mixed	3	3	0	0

When the findings are classified according to the manner in which desegregation was accomplished there is some indication that whites who chose desegregated programs may have had favorable attitudes to start with, but self-selection generally does not seem to have resulted in more positive findings for black or white volunteers or for black children in integrated neighborhoods in comparison with segregated peers. Findings are contradictory regardless of whether desegregation was "natural," mandatory, or voluntary.

4. Do other qualities of the neighborhood or school setting affect attitudinal outcomes?

Among the studies reviewed here desegregation in the South, more often than desegregation in the North, was found to be negative in its effects on children's interracial attitudes. But this geographical difference may be a function of the decade or particular location in which the studies were conducted.

In Oak Ridge, Tennessee, in the 1950s both segregated and desegregated white teenagers showed increasing prejudices — an indication that the climate of the community or times, rather than interracial contact, was affecting attitudes. On the other hand, white students with pro-desegregation parents showed a decrease in prejudice over the same time span (Whitmore, 1956; Campbell, 1956).

As we have seen, a hostile Northern community also proved to be an unfavorable setting according to the findings of Barber (1968). In Boston suburbs Useem (1971) found marked differences in attitudes toward METCO among the eight high schools she studied, differences she attributed to idiosyncratic community as well as school factors.

A school staff committed to the promotion of favorable race relations is probably a key factor in many happily desegregated schools in addition to the preschool studied by Crooks (1970). In a study of 33 interracial sixth-grade classrooms in Boston we found a significant relation between the cross-racial friendliness of white children and their teacher's fairness, according to the ratings of observers (St. John and Lewis, 1973). Another favorable school factor noted by researchers is the absence of within-school segregation. Thus one study found that with proportion black held constant, pupils' racial attitudes were more favorable in schools with racially balanced classrooms (Koslin et al., 1972a).

5. Do characteristics of individual children condition the effect of school desegregation on their attitudes?

Age. Positive, negative, and mixed findings have been reported for all age levels, but positive findings are somewhat more frequently reported for younger white children and for older blacks. Moreover, the few studies that compare attitudes across age groups find more favorable reactions to desegregation among younger children. Thus in a Hartford summer program observed seating was more interracial at the elementary than secondary level (Aronson and Noble, 1966). Following one year in a busing program in Boston 60% of the black mothers were "unreservedly in favor of busing" children in grades 1—3, but the higher the grade the more frequently did

Grade Level

Direction of Findings		Preschool	Elementary	Junior High	Senior High
Whites	+	2	3	1	5
	−		2	4	5
	0		4		2
	Mixed	1	3	1	1
Blacks	+		1	2	4
	−	1	5	2	2
	0		3		2
	Mixed	1	3		2

mothers report that their children had encountered prejudice (Teele and Mayo, 1969). On the other hand, in Indianapolis high schools seniors reported more friendly interracial contact than did freshmen (Patchen and Davidson, 1973).

Sex.   Yarrow, Campbell, and Yarrow (1958) noted that "desegregation holds the greatest initial hazards for Negro girls," and this seems to be supported by most research on the subject. A number of the studies reviewed here found less favorable cross-racial attitudes for black girls than black boys.[8] However, there is no consistency in reports of the interaction of sex and school race on the friendship behavior of black children. Some find that after desegregation black girls became more in-group and black boys less so[9] and some report the opposite finding.[10] On the other hand, among whites it appears to be boys who feel most threatened by desegregation. Not only are their attitudes more prejudiced than those of white girls, but they become more in-group in a minority group situation.[11]

Social Class.   Social class is controlled in some fashion in almost half of the studies reviewed here. But only a few of the researchers separate children according to their social class background when they examine the effect of desegregation on racial attitudes. Significant interactions among these variables have been found,[12] and there is some indication that the middle class benefit more from desegregation[13] but the matter needs further study.

Another topic that deserves study is whether the relative SES of desegregated blacks and whites affects growth of mutual tolerance. In Boston we found that social class congruity was a very significant factor in interracial friendships in sixth-grade classrooms.[14]

One variable that has historically been closely associated with social status among blacks is skin color. As noted above, Porter

reports that light-skinned children showed more white preference in desegregated settings, whereas dark-skinned children
showed the opposite tendency, preferring their own race in the
desegregated schools and choosing white dolls in the segregated
schools. However, a later replication of this study finds that
skin color is losing its importance (Sanders, 1971).

Achievement Level. Singer (1966) reported that although the
relationship between integration and tolerance was generally
positive, highly intelligent, segregated children were the most
tolerant of all. On the other hand, the most intelligent, integrated black girls were the least tolerant. Such interaction of
intelligence, racial attitudes, and school race may, however,
have been a function of self-selection of certain families into the
neighborhood schools she studied.

Useem (1971) found that grade average and placement in the
honors program was significantly related to favorable attitudes
toward METCO among white high school students. However,
the downwardly mobile (those of high SES in the noncollege
track) were the most hostile. Similarly, Lombardi (1962), who
reported no overall effect of desegregation on attitudes in a
Maryland high school, found that loss of status through decreasing grades was associated with increased hostility to incoming
blacks.

*6. Finally, does restriction of the sample of studies to those
with the most careful methodology reveal any trends in the
direction of findings?*

Many of the studies listed in Charts A-8 and A-9 were larger
studies focused on independent variables other than desegregation or on outcomes other than racial attitudes. Thus the collec-
tion of the data here reported was incidental to other objectives,
and the measurement of attitudes did not receive prime attention
in the design of the study. But when we examine the findings of

those researchers whose prime objective was studying the effect of desegregation on racial attitudes and who gave most careful attention to design and instrumentation, the evidence is nevertheless conflicting. For instance, among the studies of the attitudes of white children seven are outstanding in methodology but reveal no clear pattern in the direction of findings.

Study	Region	Grade Level	Direction of Findings
Porter (1971)	Boston	Preschool	+ −
Singer (1966)	New York	Elementary	+ −
Walker (1968)	Florida	Elementary	+ −
Webster (1961)	California	Junior High	−
Campbell (1956)	Tennessee	High School	−
Lombardi (1962)	Maryland	High School	0
Useem (1971)	Boston	High School	+

In sum, comparative studies of the racial attitudes of segregated and desegregated school children are inconclusive. Findings are inconsistent and mixed regardless of whether student's racial attitudes or friendship choice was the object of study, regardless of whether desegregation was by neighborhood or busing, voluntary or mandatory, and regardless of whether the study design was cross-sectional or longitudinal. There is some indication, however, that for black children desegregation appears more beneficial if attitudes rather than friendship behavior is the criterion and that experimental design reveals more deterioration in white attitudes than do other designs. Younger children appear to benefit from desegregation somewhat more often than older children. A hostile community or school climate seems to account for negative findings in several cases. Among characteristics of individual children that appear to be associated with the attitudinal outcome of desegregation, three variables—sex, loss of academic status, and racial congruity in social class background—seem especially worthy of further study.

4. CASE STUDIES OF DESEGREGATED SCHOOLS

In addition to the studies listed in Charts A-8 and A-9, several studies describe the degree of acceptance or cleavage in racially mixed schools without making any comparisons between subjects according to length or degree of exposure or previous experience in mixed schools. These case studies use attitudinal and sociometric scales such as those described above, as well as reports of observers and estimates of the degree of participation of minority group children in various school activities. The chief contribution of such studies to an understanding of the effects of school desegregation is evidence of the great range in interracial acceptance from community to community.

In one California community of Anglo- and Mexican-Americans, an investigator found ethnic cleavage in choice of friends which increased with age and reached 90% by the sixth grade (Parsons, 1965). Similarly, in a newly desegregated high school in Oak Park, Michigan, friendship choices were to their own group for 93% of the white students and 81% of the black students, but choices of fellow students as co-workers on preparations for a school dance or as representatives to a high school meeting were less in-group (Gordon, 1966).

In-Group Choice (%)

	Black	White
As friends	81%	93%
As fellow workers	55	71
As representatives	40	84

Almost half of the secondary school black "desegregators" studied by Chesler and Segal (1967) felt that they had encountered considerable resentment and hostility from white classmates, though in the northern part of the state (Alabama) the response was positive one-third of the time. In Georgia, a strong sex bias in participation in activities in 16 desegregated high schools was reported. In all, 72% of black males but only 49% of black females were enrolled in extracurricular activities, and 39% of males and 66% of females said white students had never asked them to participate (Hall and Gentry, 1969).

In recent years, with the implementation of court orders against dual school systems, racial cleavage in desegregated schools has reached serious proportions in many southern communities. The Lemberg Center for the Study of Violence reported that between 1967 and 1969 the proportion of race-related civil disorders taking place in schools and colleges rose from 11% (29 events) to 58% (472 events) of all disorders. Over half of these were in elementary and secondary schools, but whether the protagonists were parents, teachers, or students is not indicated (Baskin, 1971).

In the spring of 1972 a series of conferences was called by officials of the National Educational Association to investigate reports of widespread harassment of black teachers and students in desegregating systems in the South. A survey for the Southern Regional Council (Dorr, 1972) found that southern newspapers during the 1970–1971 school year reported over 4000 suspended and expelled students, and nearly 100 fights resulting in several deaths and dozens of people being hospitalized. The occasion was often the closing of a formerly all-black school, the firing or demotion of a black teacher or administrator, or the lack of black representation on school boards, students councils, teams, or social affairs.

On the other hand, a study of 252 randomly selected southern school districts by the Resource and Management Corporation for the Office of Education found that the racial climate of schools improved significantly during that same 1970–1971 year. This finding was based on over 9000 interviews with principals, teachers, and students in 14 southern states (Lynn, 1972).

In spite of the seeming contradiction, both reports should probably be accepted more or less at face value. The year 1970–1971 saw the inception of real desegregation in the most diehard sections of the South. It would be surprising if the process were without initial tension. Just as most motorists arrive at their destination unscathed in spite of an alarming accident rate for the nation, so too most school systems are apparently achieving desegregation without manifest violence, in spite of a rate of incidents that calls for serious preventative action. It is also surely true that quiet intimidation and humiliation often goes on under a cover of "improved racial climate."[15]

Planned desegregation by busing in northern communities is reported to result in more interracial acceptance than is usual in desegregating southern schools or in naturally nonsegregated northern schools. In Ann Arbor, Michigan, over 60% of transferred pupils and their parents reported favorable reactions at the end of the first year of the project (Carrigan, 1969). In Berkeley, California, 81% of mothers of bused children and 65% of mothers of receiving children said that the one-year-old program had been good for their children (Jonsson, 1966). In Evanston, Illinois after four years of desegregation a questionnaire to a sample of black parents found almost all in favor

(Hsia, 1971). In Hartford the percentage of Project Concern children receiving one or more mutual friendship choices from suburban host children was 67% ''to eat lunch with,'' 60% ''to go to a movie with,'' and 58% to ''work on a school project with.'' The percentage who indicated to interviewers a desire to remain in the project was higher in each grade from 36% in grade 2 to 93% in grade 5 (Mahan, 1968). In a large New York City open enrollment project every bused child was selected as a good or very good friend by at least one resident child in 80% of the classes, while 70% of resident and 90% of bused children said they liked the program (Fox, 1966). Finally, in Boston suburbs, 88% of white high school students said they were favorable to the METCO program in their schools, and 74% of the black students at the beginning of the school year (63% six months later) said that a majority of white students had been friendly (Useem, 1971; Armor, 1972a). A recent study of 12 Indianapolis high schools finds the net impact of interracial experience positive for both races (Patchen and Davidson, 1973).[16]

Thus in some communities desegregation is apparently followed by extreme racial cleavage; in other communities cleavage seems to be relatively minor. However, as a caution against too easy acceptance of the evidence on minority group assimilation, whether in the form of self-reports or the reports of observers, a finding by Hope (1967) in Syracuse, New York, deserves note. When 314 nonwhite and 342 white students entered two elementary and two junior high schools for the first time following a school board decision to desegregate, Hope asked the students themselves, their classroom teachers, and participant observers to rate the peer group acceptance of these new students. Quite different ratings were assigned by the three groups. Thus according to the pupils themselves, both blacks and whites assimilated better in the majority white junior high schools than in the majority black schools. According to teachers, whites assimilated somewhat better in white schools, blacks better in black schools. But according to observers whites assimilated *much* better in white schools and blacks *much* better in black schools.

5. ALLPORT'S THESIS

This review of research on racial attitudes and behavior in schools indicates that desegregation sometimes reduces prejudice and promotes interracial friendship and sometimes promotes, instead, stereotyping and interracial cleavage and conflict. An outcome so variable must be affected by circumstances other than the mere fact of desegregation.

Twenty years ago Allport (1954) concluded on the basis of existing evidence that contact between ethnic groups leads to reduced prejudice only if such contact is prolonged, is between equals in the pursuit of common goals, and enjoys the sanction of those in authority. On the surface these conditions appear to be satisfied for children attending classes together: they are in sustained contact authorized by the school board and superintendent, are in pursuit of the common goal of an education, and are equal in their status as pupils.

Reflection suggests, however, that classroom contact is often short run, competitive, and between unequals, and, though formally sanctioned, may be informally resented and bypassed by those in authority. Thus most experiments in desegregation are too new to have as yet permitted sustained contact. Official sanction for desegregation does not assure conditions favorable to real integration in those schools in which principals or teachers are personally biased. Inequality in children's ascribed characteristics (SES and academic preparation) often handicaps their equal status as pupils.

The interconnection between academic and friendship behavior may be especially close and may explain why school desegregation often does not bring growth in either respect. On the one hand, children who are unequally prepared to compete academically may maintain social distance from each other. On the other hand, social distance may prevent the less well prepared from overcoming their academic handicap.

A more detailed consideration of situational factors that affect intergroup attitudes and behaviors in desegregated schools is reserved for Chapter 5.

NOTES

1. Elizabeth Useem, Roger Riffer, and Nancy Riffer made valuable comments on an early draft of this chapter.
2. For reviews of this literature, see Allport (1954); Proshansky (1966); Porter (1971).
3. For example, Allport (1954); Clark (1955).
4. Bird, Monachesi, and Burdick (1952); Frenkel-Brunswik and Havel (1953); Mosher and Scodel (1960).
5. For an earlier review of research in this area, see Carithers (1970).
6. Pettigrew et al. (1973) have identified serious methodological weaknesses in Armor's study and argue convincingly that increase in separatist ideology should not be interpreted as pure loss.
7. Such studies include Criswell (1939); Lundberg and Dickson (1952); St. John (1964 and 1969).
8. Singer (1966); McPartland (1968); Lewis (1971); Armor (1972); Patchen and Davidson (1973).
9. Gottlieb and TenHouten (1965).
10. McWhirt (1967); Lewis (1971).
11. Gottlieb and TenHouten (1965); Singer (1966); Dentler and Elkins (1967); Porter (1971); Useem (1971); Patchen and Davidson (1973); Silverman and Shaw (1973).
12. For instance, Walker (1968).
13. For instance, Useem (1971).
14. St. John and Lewis (1974), but Patchen and Davidson (1973) report the opposite findings in Indianapolis high schools.
15. See Bailey (1970) for a thoughtful analysis of the causes of disruption in urban public secondary schools.
16. On the other hand, a study of open classrooms in a northern resegregated elementary school revealed increasing racial polarization with grade level (Bartel, Bartel and Grill, 1973).

"The worst thing about this school is its reputation"(white boy)

"The worst thing about this school is the colored people" (white girl)

"What seems to me really unfair is seeing people with money snob lower people" (black girl)

"The worst thing about this school is some of the teachers don't like colored people" (black girl)

"Kids need better schools" (black boy)

5. The Findings in Search of Theory

Scientific investigation of the results of school desegregation has from the first been action research and has leaned little on theory. Propositions derived from legal, philosophical, educational, or political opinion have been tested by social science methods. The findings having proved anomalous, it is high time to turn to social theory for enlightenment. But, given the multifaceted nature of the process of desegregation, it is unlikely that any one theoretical approach will bring full illumination. We must dissect the phenomenon into component parts and be eclectic in the search for clarifying concepts.

Beyond the methodological shortcomings of most research in this area, there are, I submit, three basic reasons why 20 years of study of the effect of school racial composition on children has netted such inconclusive results. First, desegregation is not a simple phenomenon, even for a single child in a single situation. Instead there are a number of dimensions to the experience, some favorable and some unfavorable. Second and third, the way in which desegregation is implemented, on the one hand, and the particular needs of individual children, on the other, may condition the outcome. If desegregated children gain in some respects but not in other respects or if gains for some children or some classrooms are counterbalanced by losses for other children or other classrooms, average gains would appear as inconsistent and statistically insignificant as they in fact do.

This chapter analyzes first the possible meanings for black children and white children of desegregated schools in contrast to segregated schools; next the essential conditions that must therefore obtain in the desegregated setting if pupils are to benefit in that regard are considered; finally, the potential impact of individual differences in predisposition for biracial schooling is discussed.

1. DIMENSIONS OF SCHOOL DESEGREGATION FOR BLACK CHILDREN[1]

The meaning of a phenomenon to the actors involved varies with the setting and the times. In the social context of the United States in the 1970s there seem to be at least nine dimensions to the meaning of school desegregation for black children. Each might be enlightened by reference to several bodies of social psychological theory. For each, several attitudinal variables would be appropriate measures of outcome. And several conditions must be met for each if desegregated pupils are to benefit. But for economy of space the discussion that follows focuses on one strand of theory, on one attitudinal outcome, and on the most essential school conditions suggested by each dimension. Chart 5-1 may be helpful in following the argument.

Symbolic Message and Sense of Control. Symbolic interactionist theory, as developed by Cooley (1902), Thomas (1931), and Mead (1934), sheds light on several dimensions of school desegregation. Its basic idea is that people live in a symbolic environment in which meanings and values shared with others guide their behavior. It is the actor's interpretation of the situation, rather than its structure or form, that is important.

Probably the most important aspect of school desegregation is the symbolic message it conveys. It was this aspect that the Supreme Court stressed in its 1954 decision. Until recently, the segregated school stood as a symbol of the powerlessness of the black community. Whether segregated by law, by administrative gerrymandering, or by discriminatory housing, schools have not been one-race because of the wishes of most black parents. Polls have testified repeatedly to their preference for integration.[2] The segregated school therefore acted as a signal to the ghetto child that he could not expect equal treatment in life, nor could he expect to control his own destiny. The message to him was, "Know your place".[3] In contrast, the desegregated school symbolized the victory of the black community in winning equal protection of the law. The black child in this school should therefore develop a stronger belief in his ability to control his environment. And indeed, as noted in Chapter 3, several researchers have found a positive relation between school percentage white and pupil's sense of control.

Even children in all-black schools might be encouraged by the knowledge that others of their racial group were free to enter schools of their own choosing. Some psychologists have made a useful distinction between belief in individual power and belief in the power of one's own group.[4] It is probably belief in one's group that is primarily affected by changes in public policy. Affirmative action by court or school board is a message to all

Chart 5-1 Dimensions of School Racial Composition

Dimension	Attitudinal Outcome	Necessary Conditions for Optimal Desegregation
Symbolic message	Sense of control	Black self-determination and share in control of school policies
Borrowed stigma-aura	Self-esteem	Equal access to high-quality school and high quality program
Relative deprivation	Morale	No discrimination by administration, teacher, or students
Roles and expectations of others	Motivation	Nonracist staff; techniques used to raise expectations for minority group students
Normative reference group	School-related norms	SES desegregation; middle class in majority; within-school integration
Cross-racial contact	Cross-racial attitudes	Early desegregation; equal status in schools; non-competitive climate; administrative leadership
Minority group position	Anxiety	Avoidance of both tokenism and uncontrolled or rapid influx; minority group protected against social threat
Cultural marginality	Group Identity	Biracial staff; curricular commitment to pluralism
Comparative reference group	Academic self-confidence	Individualization of instruction

that opportunity will no longer be limited to the majority group. In Washington D.C. and St. Louis, significant gains in black achievement followed systemwide desegregation, even though most black children remained in segregated classrooms.[5] One factor may well have been the encouragement the act of desegregation gave to the whole black community that its voice would be heard.

However, the symbolic meaning of desegregation may have changed since 1954. According to Hamilton (1972), "the traditionally understood integration movement was, in a profound sense, demeaning to many black nationalists" and "basically a pleading-beggar movement." Many militants now argue that advocates of desegregation or black parents who allow their children to be bused to majority white schools are thereby supporting black powerlessness. They are acting, say Carmichael and Hamilton (1967,pp.52–54), "on the assumption that there is nothing of value in the black community" and "that in order to have a decent education, black people must move into a white neighborhood or send their children to a white school." Moreover, black parents of children in majority white schools, being in a minority or residents of another school district, have probably even less influence on the policies of those schools than they have in the ghetto.[6] Others note that the closing of ghetto schools and demotion of black personnel, a common feature in the desegregation of southern school systems, conveys a psychological message as to the inferiority of black institutions and staff.[7]

A segregated school is thus not necessarily a symbol of powerlessness, nor is a desegregated school a symbol of powerlessness denied. The essential condition appears to be self-determination and share in educational decision-making, both on an individual and a community level. The black child who attends a racially mixed school would especially benefit on this dimension if desegregation were voluntary or were achieved through community effort, as in the case of Boston's Operation Exodus,[8] or if it led to political gains in the control of the mixed school. On the other hand, if a black community achieved control of its local school and managed it successfully, and if parents consciously chose that school over an equally available desegregated one, their children might experience a greater sense of power than former classmates who had fled the ghetto.[9]

Borrowed Stigma-Aura and Self-Esteem.   The individual's conception of himself grows out of social interaction with others and reflects their conception of him or of the group or organization with which he is identified.[10] Students share in the reputation of their school, with presumed consequences to their self-esteem. Segregated schools have historically, been inferior schools and probably still are, in spite of compensatory education and the impulse toward equal though separate status.[11] Moreover, the racial composition of a predominantly black school also tends to give it a reputation for low standards, poor equipment, and inexperienced staff—a reputation that outruns the facts and acts as a self-fulfilling prophecy.[12] The stigma (Goffman, 1963) of attending such schools might depress pupil self-esteem, and the aura of a mostly white school might raise it.

However, children's sense of their own worth would be enhanced neither by attending a low-status racially mixed school nor by attending a high-status school in which they were accorded low status relative to classmates. Both situations are common. "Natural" desegregation usually means that black children enter schools in racially changing neighborhoods. These schools are typically described by staff and older residents as "going downhill." Planned desegregation, on the other hand, focuses attention on racial differences and, unless very carefully managed, makes minority group children the object of curiosity and study, if not hostility. They are further stigmatized if they are singled out for remedial help, if they are tracked into a low-status program, or if they are the only children who arrive and leave by bus.

It is probable, though not yet adequately demonstrated, that an all-black school in a new location and beautiful building and conspicuous in the quality of its staff and program might contribute as much to the self-esteem of pupils as attendance at a high-status predominantly white school. But if significant sections of black society reflect white racism and attach even a limited stigma to being born black, it is unlikely that an all-black school, however exemplary, can avoid sharing that stigma.

Relative Deprivation and Morale. Closely related to the sense of powerlessness or stigma is the perception of one's own deprivation relative to that of another. Stouffer et al. (1949), studying this phenomenon among the American soldiers in World War II, found that morale depended on a comparison between soldiers' own situations and that of some other group with which they chose to compare themselves. Ghetto residents generally perceive that, in comparison with residents of other sections of the city, they are not getting their fair share of school resources. The effect on their children is undoubtedly frustration and lowered motivation.

Attendance at a desegregated school, however, would not always reduce perception of discrimination on the part of black pupils, any more than it would mitigate their powerlessness or stigma. In fact, their sense of deprivation in relation to the white pupils with whom they were in daily contact might be acute. Rosenberg and Simmons (1971), whose research was described in Chapter 3, found that segregated black children had little awareness of how low their family status was in societal terms. Their self-esteem was thus protected. If the SES or academic standards of the mixed school are higher than those of their former segregated school (and they often are), desegregated children may for the first time comprehend their own past deprivation. In addition, they may feel currently discriminated against if academic handicaps prevent access to certain courses, activities, or honors in the new school. On the other hand, in relation to others of their own race who remain in segregated schools, they may feel both gratification and deprivation—gratification with respect to the quality of education in the new school, deprivation with respect to separation from neighborhood friends, the long bus trip, or increased homework.[13]

Thus whether desegregation reduces sense of deprivation and raises morale for black pupils depends partly on their choice of referent group, but above all it depends on treatment in school. In view of the long history of racial discrimination in American society, perception of injustice on the part of minority people can probably be assuaged only by conditions that are for some years clearly better than equal. In predominantly black schools this means facilities, staff, and curricula that are visibly and dramatically superior; in racially balanced schools treatment of minority group pupils must perhaps be preferential to be equal in their eyes.[14]

Roles, Expectations of Significant Others, and Motivation. According to role theory, expectations are assigned to individuals on the basis of their locations in social systems.[15] But in a complex society there is great variation in specific locations and attendant role expectations. A most important role for a child is that of student, but expectations for students vary with the nature and reputation of their school and with the perspective of the viewer. Those whose expectations influence the young child most are usually members of his family, his teachers, and his neighborhood friends.

The expectations of these significant others tend to be low for the pupils of a ghetto school. Often principals, teachers, community residents (in general), and in particular parents do not believe that such a school will maintain high standards or prepare children to compete on an equal footing for college entrance or jobs. Several researchers have hypothesized and found evidence of a correlation among (1) the parent's or teacher's estimate of the ability of a child, (2) the child's perception of such estimates, (3) the child's rating of his own ability, and (4) the child's actual performance.[16] It is probable that children would not be unaffected by low expectations for themselves as a group and as individuals as long as they remain in the typical ghetto school.

In a desegregated school, however, a black child does not necessarily escape the depressing effect of low expectations of others. The expectations of staff and pupils here may be low not for all, as perhaps is the case in the ghetto school, but merely for the "culturally deprived," the bused, or the black pupil. The effect would be all the more devastating. The fact that in such a school his parent's expectations for him are usually high could be in fact dysfunctional for a child, suggests Katz (1967), if his anxiety is thereby raised and he is not supported by equally reassuring expectations (and help) from his teachers.

There are techniques for raising the expectations of teachers and peers for the academic performance of minority group children. Cohen and co-workers (1970) have demonstrated in laboratory experiments with interracial teams that public demonstration of the competence of black subjects increases their assertive behavior and white partners' expectations for them.[17] However, sustained high expectations on the part of staff can probably have a facilitating effect on pupil motivation even in a predominantly black school, as evidenced by the extraordinary gains of pupils in the New York Demonstration Guidance program[18] and the initial gains for pupils in the Banneker schools in St. Louis.[19]

Peers as Reference Group and School-Related Norms. Another dimension of school desegregation is exposure to classmates whose ways of thinking and acting may be different from those of a child's family or neighborhood friends.

How great will the influence of the new values and behavior patterns be? According to differential association theory, this depends on the degree of association.[20] The larger the group in a classroom, the greater the statistical probability that its norms will be adopted by all. But according to reference group theory, the outcome cannot be predicted by simple ratios: who influences whom depends on the reward structure in society and in the local setting.[21]

The pupils of a ghetto school are usually reported to be deficient in varying degrees in school-related interests, motivation, and self-discipline.[22] *If* white children are less deficient in these respects, and *if* we accept the proposition that the greater the proportion of any social group in a school the more likely that its norms and attitudes dominate and are adopted by members of the other groups, *then* we would predict improved attitudes for black children who move to a school in which white pupils are in the majority. The viability of this assumption rests on at least three (somewhat questionable) assumptions:

1. The first is that the norms of the white children involved are indeed more achievement oriented than those of the desegregating black children. But a review by Proshansky and Newton (1968) suggests that black and white children differ less in motivation than in the expectation of achieving their goals.[23] Furthermore, it is probable that differences in other norms important for achievement are a function of social class rather than race. Only if the racially balanced school were more middle class than the imbalanced school would desegregation increase exposure to achievement-oriented norms.

2. The second unwarranted assumption is that in a bi-racial school black and white children are integrated into a single social group. But in many schools racial groups are separated either formally through academic tracking and academic restrictions on extracurricular activities or informally through racial pride and hostility.[24] Homogenization of values and norms

would occur within rather than between racial groups in this situation.

3. The third questionable assumption is that those in the minority accept those in the majority as their normative reference group. But sociological theory suggests that individuals who lack means of realizing status in the dominant society will reject the standards of that society and will seek status among peers who do likewise.[25] Until the day when there is full equality in the status of blacks and whites in American society, some racial separation in the reference group behavior of youth is to be expected. However, the reward structure and climate of the local school could also affect the degree of separation and cross-racial influence.

Thus it is social class desegregation rather than racial desegregation that holds the greatest potential for affecting children's norms and values. Whether desegregated children actually adopt the norms of middle-class peers depends on the degree of exposure to them as well as on the intergroup climate of the school. Whether the new norms are "better" or more " functional" or more "adaptive" depends, of course, on one's point of view.

Cross-Racial Contact and Cross-Racial Attitudes.   Attendance at a biracial school exposes a child not only to the attitudes *of* the other group but also to a change in his own attitudes *toward* the other group. The hypothesis that interracial contact leads to reduced prejudice has received confirmation from research with adults and in other institutional areas. The important conditions, according to Allport (1954), are that contact be prolonged, equal status, in pursuit of common goals, and institutionally sanctioned. We would therefore expect black and white children to develop favorable attitudes toward each other after some months or years together, provided that (1) they are fairly similar in social class and academic background and in the status they are accorded in the desegregated school, (2) there is no real clash of interests or tense intergroup competition and (3) the school administration shows no racial bias and favors full integration rather than mere desegregation.

The first precondition for amelioration of prejudice, that contact be prolonged, has not yet been met in many desegregated schools. As we saw in Chapter 4, many studies measure changes in racial attitudes over the first six months of contact. But it takes time to get beyond the initial discomfort and tension of an interracial situation.[26] Several of the studies reviewed found evidence that long-term desegregation had a beneficial effect on attitudes.

The second precondition, that contact be equal status, is also seldom fully realized. Black and white children may be unequally prepared to be successful students or may be accorded unequal status in the peer group because of differential family background. It should be noted, however, that this condition for prejudice-reducing contact, equality of status, runs counter to one of the conditions stipulated in the previous section as necessary if desegregation is to have normative benefit: adopting the norms of the peers will be functional for a child's school achievement, I suggested, only if those peers are *more* middle class in background and display *more* achievement-oriented behavior than himself. What is perhaps necessary to satisfy both conditions is that staff treat lower-class newcomers with respect and equality so that they feel free to adopt middle-class norms through "anticipatory socialization".[27] Friendship and reduction in prejudice can then follow.

Administrative sanction is probably the most important precondition of prejudice-reducing contact in schools. If central office staff is determined that integration shall be complete, the status of all school children made equal, and racial competition avoided, the other necessary ingredients of healthy biracial schools probably will follow.[28]

Thus although an important dimension of school desegregation is the opportunity it affords for interracial contact, several other important conditions must be met if such contact is to lead to interracial friendliness rather than to interracial conflict or increased prejudice.

The presumption for each of the six dimensions so far considered is in favor of the desegregated school. There are three other dimensions for which the presumption is in favor of the segregated school.

Minority Group Position and Anxiety. The black child who is desegregated is usually a newcomer in an unfamiliar setting, a "sociological stranger",[29] and, typically, in a racial minority. His consequent fear of social threat, be it of mere rejection or of physical harm, will be mild or severe depending on the community, the circumstances surrounding desegregation, his ego strength, and his prior interracial experience.[30] Katz argues that "covert reactions to social threat would constitute an important source of intellectual impairment" (1968, p. 256) since anxiety, distraction, and emotion all lower efficacy and since the threatened child might try not to excel in order to avoid arousing further resentment.[31]

Even when the social threat is mild or nonexistent, the black child in a majority white classroom may not be able to forget his color. He cannot avoid perception of his racial status and of the prejudices of some whites.[32] Rather than being simply a pupil, a boy or a girl, he must play the role of representing his race, its strengths, and its agenda. An evaluation of the ABC program (described in Chapter 3) that places disadvantaged black students in independent middle-class schools quotes a senior who wrote, "I am tired of being under the microscope explaining things which pertain to my people".[33] Pierce (1968) writes, "I believe our society will be integrated when no one has to think any time during the day about his color. . . . A white cannot possibly comprehend the amount of psychic energy that is required to be a Negro" (p. 24).

The effect of black/white ratios on race relations has been the object of more theoretical speculation than systematic study. Allport (1954) suggested that the rapid influx and growing density of a minority population "is not in itself a sufficient principle to explain prejudice. What it seems to accomplish is the aggravation of whatever prejudice exists" (p. 229). According to Blalock (1967), conditions will be most favorable for a minority group if its numbers are sufficient to exert pressure without constituting a power threat to the majority group. This means perhaps the avoidance of less than 15% and more than 40% of black children in a school.[34]

Planned desegregation need not mean, for the black child, being in a racial minority in his classroom, but it usually does (and in fact must, if the benefits of several other dimensions of desegregation are to be realized) and so exposes him to a degree of social threat. Whether the threat is mild or severe, whether he responds with anxiety or aggressiveness, whether the situation improves or deteriorates after the first weeks of school will depend, theory suggests, on black/white ratios and the rapidity of change in such ratios, on the interracial climate of the school, on staff support, as well as on his own interpersonal skill.

Cultural Marginality and Group Identity.   The black child in a white classroom faces more than social threat. He is also a marginal man, bridging two social worlds, and his loyalty to and identity with his own racial group may be weakened.[35] To the extent that there are real differences in values and mores between these worlds, the child may be torn between feeling he both should and should not, in Hamilton's words (1968) "attempt to be a carbon copy of the culture and ethos of another racial and ethnic group." Pettigrew (1969) suggests that the values of black and white families are more similar than either realize. Desegregated children have the opportunity of making this discovery, and their values will converge still further as a result. Nevertheless, faced with a choice between separation and acculturation, the child risks both estrangement from his own racial group and rejection by the other group, as well as confusion as to his identity and resultant normlessness.[36]

As reported in Chapter 3, Crain (1971) found that black adults whose childhood experience with integration was inconsistent (where neighborhood or elementary school or high school was integrated and the other two were segregated) had lowest self-esteem and sense of control, presumably because they had not been able to develop a stable identity. Rosenberg and Simmons (1971) found that in a black setting children's self-esteem was not lower if they came from a separated or never-married family. In white schools, on the other hand, where this family type is more stigmatized, such children had lower self-esteem. They conclude that "consonant social context" protects an individual's self-esteem whereas a "dissonant context" threatens his self-esteem.

It should be noted, however, that in a real sense many black children experience marginality in all-black schools. The culture of the school is typically that of white, middle-class America and does not encourage healthy racial identity. The cure for marginality in schools of whatever racial mix is removal of racist overtones from the curriculum, provision for cultural emphasis on the Afro-American experience, and staff integration. But, according to Allport (1954), pluralism cannot be mandated: "What is needed is freedom for both assimilation and for pluralism to occur according to the needs and desires of the minority group itself" (p. 240).

Comparative Reference Group and Academic Self-Confidence. Peers serve as comparative as well as normative reference group. In other words, individuals not only adopt the norms of peers, but also take the achievement of peers as a standard against which to measure their own success.[37] When a child moves from a segregated to an integrated school, he may leave a relatively protected colony and face what Pettigrew (1967) calls "the opportunity for cross-racial evaluation" or what Pierce (1968) calls "the incessant burden of proving himself to the satisfaction of the white majority" (p. 24). Katz (1964) believes that such cross-racial comparisons can have both a high incentive value and a high informational value. The black child wants to succeed in the interracial classroom and there learns that all whites are not better students than he. Moreover, the level and pace of instruction may be more stimulating than that in his previous school.

But the advantage of realistic competition can be offset by fear of failure. Katz goes on to postulate that in view of generally inadequate early training, either at home or in segregated schools, a desegregated child will often have a low probability of success. In addition, he may suffer from unrealistic feelings of inferiority. He is therefore not able to live up to expectations of his parents and his own motivation to do well. Anxiety and lowered self-concept follow.

In the study of Baltimore school children referred to previously, Rosenberg and Simmons (1971) report these findings:

> Black children in white secondary schools obtain higher marks than those in black schools, but although high marks are conducive to high self-esteem, black children in integrated schools still have lower self-esteem than segregated blacks. We reasoned that the black children in the white schools are comparing themselves unfavorably with either the white children in their schools (interaction group) or with whites in general (non-membership group); they are not comparing themselves with those of most black children (membership group). (P. 137)

Kemper (1968) argues that coincidence of audience and of normative and comparative reference groups is most facilitative for achievement. Tension and separation between racial groups probably prevents such coincidence in many schools, with the results that black students maintain their own norms and behavior patterns but perform to a largely white audience and measure their success by white standards. The outcome is probably deleterious to both self-confidence and achievement.

In a series of laboratory experiments Katz (1968) demonstrated that black subjects perform better in a biracial situation when the threat of punishment is mild,[38], when they do not expect to be judged against white norms,[39] when the task is not defined as a test of intelligence,[40] and when the chance of success is believed to be slightly better than even. Thus the factors that will probably determine whether the desegregated classroom is, on balance, academically facilitating rather than threatening are lack of interracial tension and either initial similarity in achievement level of black and white children or else supportiveness of school staff, availability of school academic policies that favor overcoming handicaps, avoidance of competition, and above all individualization of instruction.[41] But, as in the case of other dimensions of desegregation, many of these same factors could transform a ghetto school into a setting in which a strong yet realistic academic motivation is fostered.

2. DIMENSIONS OF SCHOOL DESEGREGATION FOR WHITE CHILDREN

There are as many dimensions to school desegregation for white children as for black children, but they are discussed in less detail here.

The pupils in a segregated white school are less aware than those in a segregated black school of their participation in the symbolic denial of the American democratic ideal of equality of all citizens. In the North, until recently, distance from the ghetto and a conspiracy of silence have quarantined most white children from realization of the existence and nature of ghetto schools. This is no longer true except for very young children. The desegregation controversy and its treatment by press and television have brought home to suburban children a realization of their privileged position and exposed them to a false sense of superiority. Rescued from ignorance, they are now exposed to the more dangerous rationalizations of their elders and to a sense of de facto implication in an institution which denies the democratic ideals they are being taught to revere. Thus this symbolic dimension of segregation can harm white children through the encouragement of hypocrisy and prejudice. In contrast, desegregation should encourage pride in community and faith in democracy.

Other meanings of desegregation to white pupils depend very much on black-to-white ratios and on expectations for future change in ratios. As long as the proportion of black pupils is small (under 20%) and expected to remain so, there is no reason for white pupils to experience stigma, relative deprivation, social threat, marginality, or a change in norms, standards, or the expectations of their significant others. Prejudice may be reduced if black pupils are not too different in social background.

On the other hand, a school 20 to 50% black could have negative influence on white children on some dimensions. Even a majority white school may have low status; proximity to a growing ghetto or the rapid increase in the proportion of black pupils often lead to perceptions of falling standards which outrun the facts and act as a self-fulfilling prophecy. Especially if further racial change were expected, whites in schools 20 to 50% black might sense stigma, deprivation, and lowered expectations relative to pupils in all-white schools. They might overreact to such perceptions and lose interest in school; they might feel the same sense of relative deprivation in comparison with former classmates who have moved to the suburbs that blacks feel in comparing themselves with pupils in suburban schools. If they were bused to inner city schools against their will, they might feel conscripted and resentful. If staff appeared to favor black students in any way, whites would feel discriminated against and might become more antiblack. And they might experience social threat if blacks were aggressive or united. If black students were accepted as their leaders or their norms proved attractive, the values and norms of white students might be affected (white parents would say "for the worse").

Schools over 50% black would usually not benefit white pupils for the same reasons that they would not benefit black pupils. Unless extra resources were poured in, the disadvantage might here be real rather than imagined, and whites would thereby lose the "advantage" of numerical and cultural dominance. White children will be just as adversely affected as are black children by attending a school with low status in the eyes of the community, a school in which their parents and teachers have low expectations for academic accomplishment, or a school with mediocre or low academic standards. If their prior training had been strong, however, they might enjoy being "big frogs in a little pond," academically speaking.[42] But though their grades and self-esteem might thus be enhanced, objective test scores would presumably suffer.

According to the theory of differential association discussed earlier, the larger the percentage of black children in a school, the more likely that white children will adopt their attitudes and behaviors. But this does not warrant the conclusion that the more blacks in a school the less achievement-oriented will be the attitudes and behavior of white children. As suggested, there is probably little difference between the norms of the two groups of children, once social class is controlled, and any differences that exist are certainly not necessarily to the exclusive advantage of one racial group. For instance, studies repeatedly find that black youth report higher aspirations but show less realism or knowledge about the world of work. If white youth learned aspiration while black youth learned realism about how to achieve it, both could benefit from mutual association. Through there is the possibility that desegregation will hurt white children by exposing them to the victims of social disorganization and discrimination, there is also the likelihood that they will either resist or benefit from homogenization of norms.

The point should be made, however, that isolated white children in predominantly black schools are as liable to social threat and constricting fear as are black pioneers in predominantly white schools. The chief difference is that the former are usually low SES children in low SES schools and the latter upwardly mobile children in middle-class schools. The realistic risk of physical molestation might therefore be greater for the white child in the ghetto, the risk of ostracism by the "well-bred" greater for the black child in suburbia. Either social situation is stressful; whether it results in increased hostility or lowered self-confidence would depend on many factors, especially the child's basic personality structure and family support, on the one hand, and the understanding and protection of teachers, on the other.

Thus a simple change in the racial composition of their school may have many simultaneous consequences for the pupils involved. A message of discouragement or hope may be conveyed, a stigma conferred or withdrawn, a sense of relative deprivation produced or alleviated, the expectations of significant others lowered or raised, the normative reference group changed, intergroup contact narrowed or broadened, the ingroup/outgroup balance shifted, cultural identification confused or clarified, and the standard for self-evaluation downgraded or upgraded.

3. NECESSARY AND SUFFICIENT CONDITIONS

The dimensions of school desegregation just described are potentially operative for all students, but their impact could be minor or drastic depending on the manner in which desegregation is implemented and on characteristics of individual children.

The educational conditions under which desegregation is likely to have the most beneficial and least harmful outcomes for children are suggested by a consideration of its various dimensions. Though on six dimensions the presumption is that racial balance in schools would be beneficial to the children involved, in each case I believe that this would be true only if certain conditions were met. An on the three dimensions on which the presumption is the other way, the negative outcome might be avoided if circumstances were right. Desegregation should benefit children under the following conditions:

1. Desegregation, as a symbol of equality affirmed and powerlessness denied, should increase black sense of control and white appreciation of democracy, *provided* it is achieved through individual or community self-determination and is freely chosen by the families involved, and provided black parents share in the control of school policies.

2. Desegregation should reduce stigma and enhance the self-esteem of black pupils *provided* that it is to a school of higher status and provided they are not placed in low-status programs or classes in the new school.

3. Desegregation, by reducing sense of deprivation relative to pupils in other schools, should raise the morale of black pupils, *provided* they do not feel deprived in relation to majority white pupils in the new school.

4. Desegregation may raise the expectations of significant others and so the motivation of black pupils, *provided* such expectations are from staff as well as parents, for those whose initial performance is low as well as high, and for white and black students alike.

5. Desegregation brings association with peers from whom favorable norms may be acquired, *provided* racial desegregation means social class desegregation and does not result in official or unofficial within-school segregation.

6. Desegregation brings interracial contact which may reduce prejudice, *provided* it is continued over a number of years,

provided it is equal status and noncompetitive, and *provided* that the school administration offers firm leadership.

On the other hand, desegregation may raise the following problems:

1. Desegregation inevitably places some pupils in a minority group situation which may induce anxiety, *unless* both tokenism and rapid influx is avoided and unless the staff is firm and skillful in protecting whichever race is in the minority.

2. Desegregation exposes minority group pupils to cultural marginality and confusion as to their own identity, *unless* the staff is interracial, *unless* the curriculum recognizes the minority group culture, and *unless* there is opportunity for choice between assimilation and pluralism.

3. Desegregation allows self-evaluation against academic standards that may in some cases discourage motivation, *unless* help is available, competition is avoided, and instruction and evaluation are individualized.

Many of these conditions would also temper the potentially negative impact of majority-black schools. In fact, on several dimensions segregated black children appear to be in the stronger position. On the other dimensions it seems that only integration in racially balanced schools will realize the desired outcome.

The word *integration* as here used needs further definition. To some people the noun connotes simply the mixing, voluntary or involuntary, of people of different racial or cultural backgrounds. For this concept, *desegregation* is the term used in this book. Other interpretations of the meaning of *integration* refer to equality of opportunity, to equality of social status, to assimilation, or to its opposite, the acceptance of cultural diversity.[43]

An interesting study by Marascuilo and Dagenais (1972) asked Berkeley high school seniors to choose among eight definitions the ones that "come closest to your own feeling about integration.'' All racial groups rejected the ideas of forced mixing or assimilation and gave high priority to free association on the basis of mutual interest, to equality of social status, and to pluralism (''open acceptance of another person and his racial and cultural heritage''). A racial difference appeared in regard to Webster's definition, ''the incorporation or inclusion into society on the basis of equal membership, of people who differ on some characteristic (like race).''[44] Both Asian and black students (but especially blacks) rejected this definition more than did white students. The authors suggest that to minority group students the dictionary definition implies giving up their own cultural and racial heritage.

The analysis in this chapter of the social-psychological dimensions of school segregation and of the conditions under which desegregation would confer benefits suggests that the Berkeley young people are right in their support of free association over forced mixing, of equality of social status over mere equality of opportunity, and of pluralism over assimilation. It is integration in this sense that seems a necessary condition of desirable desegregation.

4. INDIVIDUAL DIFFERENCES

The impact of school desegregation is conditioned not only by the local situation and the manner in which it is implemented, but also by characteristics of the individual children involved. The research reviewed in Chapters 2, 3, and 4 suggest that among the relevant individual factors are age, sex, ego strength, academic ability, and SES. On the average, those who are most favorably affected by desegregation seem to be the young children, the boys, the self-confident, the high achievers, and the middle class. Their opposite numbers may benefit more from segregated schools or, if desegregated, probably require more support from teachers to keep the experience from being counterproductive.

Age. Desegregation is probably more beneficial if it is begun in early elementary years. Academic development is cumulative, and the gap in achievement between minority and majority group children usually widens with age. Thus according to several investigators the younger the age the greater the growth in achievement. There is also some evidence that desegregation is socially easier in early grades. Young children are aware of racial differences and stereotypes, but racial prejudices and fears are less firmly established than in older children. School situations in which attitudes deteriorate or open conflict occurs are usually at the junior high or secondary level and follow segregated early schooling.

Sex. Among blacks the social threat of desegregation is almost universally reported to be greater for girls than boys. Several studies reviewed in Chapter 3 indicate that the aspirations, self-concept, and assurance of black girls was lower in desegregated than in segregated schools.[45] Other studies have found that black girls show less favorable interracial attitudes and greater own-group preference than the other race-sex groups. Among whites, on the other hand, the social threat of desegregation appears greater for boys than girls.

We can only conjecture as to the reasons for such sex differences in reaction to mixed schooling. The importance of athletics to boys and beauty to girls in the Adolescent Society studied by Coleman (1961) provides one clue. In racially mixed schools the athletic skills of many black males give them self-confidence and prestige which will be lacking for their sisters as long as feminine beauty is judged by the standards of white society.[46] It is also possible that black athletes may be seen as heros by white girls but as rivals by white boys. Black girls probably resent any friendship between their brothers and white girls and (consciously or unconsciously reacting against the historic exploitation of black women by white men) reject on their part any advances from white boys.[47]

Mental Health.   Desegregation may be more beneficial to pupils already high in ego strength and self-confidence. A number of psychologists have pointed out that individual differences in temperament, cognitive traits, and family experiences will result in idiosyncratic variation in reactions to desegregation.[48] Many studies have found more symptoms of personality disorders and anxiety among black children than white children, and Katz (1967) demonstrated in several laboratory experiments that anxiety tends to be especially high with white partners or white testers. Wessman (1969) studied the progress of highly selected minority group boys in independent schools (Project ABC). Academic success over two years was related to initial scores on a personality inventory indicating that the student was serious, motivated, responsible, conscientious. Such outcomes may seem self-evident, but they also suggest that some children will require special consideration when a school system desegregates.

Achievement Level.   Students of high ability or achievement level are generally more ready to benefit from desegregation. According to Katz' (1964) model, a biracial classroom is socially facilitating to high achievers but threatening to low achievers, whose probability of success is likely to be low and who often fear failure. He found previously low-achieving boys to be more self-critical and to have higher test anxiety than high-achieving boys, even when there was no objective difference in their current task performance. Several studies referred to in Chapter 2 found that pupils with low initial academic ability made few or no gains when desegregated.[49] As to the differential effect of achievement level on interracial friendship, we found in Boston that black sixth graders were significantly more friendly to and popular with white classmates if their initial achievement level was high.[50] Among whites achievers tend to be the least prejudiced; their status is not threatened.[51]

But downward mobility in academic status is associated with increased hostility.[52]

Family SES. A child's social and economic background affects his adjustment to desegregation in the same way that his academic background does. In general, black children of low SES are least ready socially and academically to adjust well to biracial schools and children of high SES are most ready. This generalization is supported by the findings of a number of the studies reviewed in this book.

Conclusion. This list of variables is not meant to be exhaustive but to suggest that there are identifiable characteristics of children which condition the benefits of desegregation for them. Other variables that probably affect reaction to desegregation include physical appearance (size, strength, maturity, charm), previous interracial experience, and racial attitudes of parents.[53] For white children similar propositions could be developed as to which children would probably benefit or suffer from, for example, reverse busing to ghetto schools. For any ethnic group the expected within-group differences would be a matter of central tendencies, not categorical differences. Obviously many older, lower-class children will respond better to an interracial classroom than many younger or middle-class children, though on the average this is probably not so.

I am not suggesting here that desegregation is only for the strong. It is true that those with any type of handicap are poorly prepared for a situation that is strange, stressful, or competitive, but in many settings this description might fit the segregated school better than the desegregated one. Nor am I suggesting that there are only negative reasons for preferring a black school. For certain children at certain stages in their development a black school might represent a great challenge or fill a great need. But in any case, in view of the number of relevant variables and their possible permutations and interaction effects,

readiness for the stress or need for the challenge of desegregation appears to be a very individual matter.

A fourfold table is the most graphic way of conceptualizing
the probably joint influence of individual and situational differences on the outcomes of school desegregation. Not forgetting
that desegregation is, as this chapter has argued, a many-sided
phenomenon and for any one child in any one situation, favorable in some respects and unfavorable in other respects, nevertheless on balance the outcome will probably be as follows:

		Individual Characteristics	
		Unfavorable	Favorable
Desegregated	Unfavorable	Prognosis poor	?
Situation	Favorable	?	Prognosis good

If most of the conditions stipulated above are met, then for
those children who are well equipped (according to the characteristics I have named), the academic and attitudinal outcomes
of desegregation will be favorable. If the conditions are not met
and children are not equipped, then it is probable that desegregation will produce no benefit and possibly much harm. In the
other two cases the outcome remains in doubt and probably
hinges on unusually favorable qualities of either the individual
or the situation.

The discussion in this chapter is admittedly speculative.
Though supported by strands of social-psychological theory and
not contradicted by the evidence reviewed in previous chapters,
the propositions here outlined have yet to be tested rigorously.

Should large public funds now be expended on new research? How should such research be conducted? And while awaiting the results, what should public policy be? To these questions the next chapter is addressed.

NOTES

1. Section 1 of Chapter 5 is a much revised version of a paper that appeared in H. Walberg and A. Kopan, eds., *Urban Education Today: Rethinking Theory and Practice,* Jossey-Bass, San Francisco 1972.

2. Brink and Harris (1964); Campbell and Schuman (1968), Marx (1967); and Goldman (1970).

3. See Pettigrew (1964).

4. Gurin et al. (1969).

5. Hansen (1960); Stallings (1959).

6. See Handlin (1966), and Piven and Cloward (1967), on the political suicide of desegregation. A number of researchers report that black parents are less active in school affairs following desegregation of the system or their children. See Prichard (1969a).

7. Entin (1972). Poussaint (1970) writes, "Since integration is nearly always a one-way street that blacks travel to a white institution, then an implied inferiority of the black man is inherent in the situation, because it is *he who must* seek out whites to better his position. This implies that only he can benefit and learn; that he has nothing to offer whites; that whites have nothing to learn from his presence" (p. 13).

8. Teele, Jackson and Mayo (1967).

9. Guttentag reports that children in Harlem's Community controlled school (IS201) blamed school failure on parents, teachers, and school rather than on self. Clark (1973) argues that decentralization and community control without control of the purse strings is hollow. Moreover, without a transition in which ghetto people are supported and trained to run their own schools, small groups will tend to dominate, and community-wide control will not be realized.

10. Cooley (1902).

11. See McCauley and Ball (1959), Coleman et al. (1966), and *National Advisory Commission on Civil Disorders* (1968).

12. Fauman (1957); Pinderhughes (1964).

13. Vanneman and Pettigrew (1972) have demonstrated the usefulness of Runciman's (1966) distinction between egotistic and fraternal deprivation in explaining racial attitudes of white adults. The distinction also clarifies the potential gains and losses to children's morale that goes with desegregation. The key in both cases is the choice of referent group. See also U.S. Commission on Civil Rights (1970).

14. Young (1964).

15. Gross, Mason, and McEachern (1958).

16. For example, see Clark (1965); Brookover et al. (1965); Davidson and Lang (1960); Schwartz and Tangri (1965); Rosenthal and Jacobson (1968).

17. Katz (1967) reports experiments with similar results.

18. Wrightstone (1960).

19. U.S. Commission (1967).

20. Sutherland (1955).

21. Shibutani (1955) and Merton (1957).

22. According to Becker (1952) and Herriot and St. John (1966), this is what teachers and principals say.

23. Preliminary analysis of Riverside data leads Gerard and Miller (1971) to question the hypothesis that minority children are different in motivation.

24. See the report of the National Association of Secondary School Principals (Bailey, 1970).

25. Merton (1957); Cohen (1955).

26. Pettigrew (1969); Pierce (1968).

27. Merton (1957).

28. See U.S. Commission on Civil Rights (1967a), p. 154, on administrative measures necessary for effective school desegregation.

29. Simmel (1950).

30. Coles (1967); and Milner (1953). See Cottle's poignant account of Harry Benjamin in *The New York Times Magazine*, 23 April 1972. The Group for the Advancement of Psychiatry (1957) predicted types of psychological stress that would be involved, including "emigration neurosis", the near-paranoid interpretation of majority-group behavior by the newcomer who expects rejection.

31. Allport (1954), under the heading, "Traits due to Victimization," analyzed the ego defenses that frequently develop among those who are socially threatened.

32. Rosenberg and Simmons (1971) found that 34% of black children in

predominantly black schools, but 51% in predominantly white schools reported having ever been teased because of race (p.27). Moreover, blacks in white schools were considerably more likely than blacks in black schools to say that "most people in America" rank blacks last (p. 37). See also Williams (1964).

33. Perry (1973).

34. Patchen and Davidson (1973) found that rapid increase in percentage of blacks in Indianapolis high schools was associated with avoidance of blacks by whites. The more power students of either race had, the more positively they acted toward the other race.

35. Stonequist (1937); Park (1950).

36. Fishman (1961).

37. Kelley (1952); Kemper (1968).

38. Katz and Greenbaum (1963).

39. Katz et al. (1964).

40. Katz et al. (1965).

41. Mahan (1968) found that Project Concern youth bused from Hartford ghettto to suburban schools benefited especially in those schools in which extra teachers were assigned to help with their academic adjustment. Pettigrew et al. (1973) point out, however, that desegregation often means a reduction rather than an increase in such supporting services. See also Frelow (1971). The evidence of Stodolsky and Lesser (1967) as to the different modal mental ability patterns of different racial groups suggest the advisability of adapting instruction in such a way as to capitalize the individual child's initial strengths and to minimize his initial weaknesses, remembering that his own style may not follow any modal racial pattern.

42. Davis (1966).

43. Handlin (1966) notes two meanings of integration, (1) openness of society and leveling of barriers, and (2) racial balance, and deplores the shift in public emphasis from (1) to (2). Pettigrew (1971) writes, "the long-term goal of integration is not a complete obliteration of cultural pluralism, of distinctive Negro ghettoes, but rather the transformation of these ghettoes from racial prisons to ethnic areas freely chosen or not chosen" (p. 323).

44. This is an adaptation of *Webster's Seventh New Collegiate Dictionary* definition.

45. Armor (1967); McPartland (1968); Denmark (1970); Carrigan (1969).

46. See Freeman, et al. (1966); Ransford (1970).

47. Grier and Cobbs (1968).

48. Ausubel (1963); Bernard (1958); and Milner (1953).

49. Denmark (1970); Purl and Dawson (1971), and Wessman (1969); on the other hand, perhaps due to "regression to the mean", Carrigan (1969) and Frary and Goolsby (1970) find greatest gains for those with low pretransfer scores.

50. St. John and Lewis (1974); for a similar finding for Indianapolis high schools, see Patchen and Davidson (1973).

51. Useem (1971). Patchen and Davidson (1973).

52. Lombardi (1962).

53. Patchen and Davidson (1973) found that the more positive their families' racial attitudes and the more interracial contacts they had had in their neighborhoods and other settings, the more friendly interaction blacks and whites report with other-race classmates in high school.

"Someday I will be out of Roxbury I hope because I don't like Roxbury" (black boy, grade 6)

"Someday I will have people trust in me and respect me" (black boy, grade 6)

"Someday I will go out to see the whol world and meat other people in it" (black girl, grade 6)

6. Alternatives and Choice: The Road Ahead[1]

School desegregation is unfinished national business. After two decades of agonizing, rhetoric, interposition, litigation, protest, and half-steps, most school systems in the South may at last be desegregated, but many schools and many children are not. In the North, there is today more racial segregation than there was in 1954.[2] And everywhere the issue continues to divide Americans. Yet at the same time there has been continued growth in commitment to integration in principle, not only by the general public[3] but also by legislators, officials, school boards, and educators, while judicial interpretation of the constitutional mandate for desegregation has expanded steadily. Therefore, though the road ahead may be rough and tortuous, it cannot circle back.

Given the political and educational importance of the topic, it is regrettable that we still know so little about the meaning of school desegregation to the pupils involved. The reason for our ignorance is that by and large theory has been undeveloped, educational experimentation limited, and research poorly designed. There is no indication, however, that we need to revise the basic hypothesis that in the long run integration benefits children. It is the implementation rather than the goal which now needs attention—how can "mere desegregation" be translated into "true integration"?

1. SUMMING UP

This book has reviewed more than 120 studies of the relation of school racial composition and the achievement, attitudes, or behavior of children. On the basis of this evidence biracial schooling must be judged neither a demonstrated success nor a demonstrated failure.

As implemented to date, desegregation has not rapidly closed the black-white gap in academic achievement, though it has rarely lowered and sometimes raised the scores of black children. Improvement has been more often reported in the early grades, in arithmetic, and in schools over 50% white, but even here the gains have usually been mixed, intermittent, or nonsignificant. White achievement has been unaffected in schools that remained majority white but significantly lower in majority black schools.

Biracial schooling is apparently not detrimental to the academic performance of black children, but it may have negative effects on their self-esteem. It is not merely academic self-concept in the face of higher standards that is threatened, but also general self-concept. In addition, desegregation apparently lowers educational and vocational aspirations. It is possible, however, to interpret a reduction of unrealistically high aspirations as an overall gain. Moreover, there is some evidence that in the long run desegregation may encourage the aspiration, self-esteem, and sense of environmental control of black youth.

The immediate effect of desegregation on interracial attitudes is sometimes positive but often negative. Thus white racism is frequently aggravated by mixed schooling. Friendship is somewhat more likely to develop among younger children or those who have been long desegregated, but at the secondary school level there is great range in the degree of racial cleavage, community to community. In some schools there is considerable friendly interaction and mutual respect. In other schools contact is minimal and interracial incidents frequent. Among blacks the most ingroup in their friendship patterns are girls and those in classes with very few of their own race. Among whites the most ingroup are boys, but the interracial behavior of both sexes is much affected by the social class congruity of the races in the school.

But although desegregation is not to date a demonstrated success, it is not yet a demonstrated failure. There is as little evidence of consistent loss as there is of consistent gain. Further, in spite of the large number of studies, various limitations in design weaken the best of them. Thus in a sense the evidence is not all in.

A very narrow range of outcomes has been studied. There have been virtually no long-term longitudinal studies with pre-desegregation and postdesegregation scores on the same tests and with subjects randomly assigned to experimental and control conditions. Nor, in lieu of random assignment, have subjects been matched with sufficient care on home background and initial ability. In many studies no attempt was made to measure family background and social class; and where the attempt was made the measurement was usually crude and undependable. Nor has school quality been controlled; in fact, virtually the only studies that have employed an experimental design have been those in which children bused to outlying schools are compared with former classmates who continued in ghetto schools. Even when sending and receiving schools are in the same system (and they often are not), they usually differ a great deal in plant, equipment, program, and the credentials of teachers. But the most serious lack in desegregation research has been inattention to the classroom process. The defensiveness of principals and teachers has precluded proper evaluation of their role in structuring the racial climate of schools. A further possible limitation to the relevance of many studies is the year in which the data were gathered. The racial climate of opinion has changed drastically over the last two decades and with it probably the meaning of desegregation. Even five-year-old findings may be dated and not necessarily representative of the current situation.

But having admitted these limitations, and fully cognizant that all the facts may not be in, I believe the evidence of wide-ranging studies is in one respect clear: school desegregation per se has no unitary or invariable effect on children. As indicated in Chapter 5, my interpretation of the mixed and inconsistent findings is twofold. First, desegregation is a multifaceted phenomenon which can be simultaneously beneficial in some respects and harmful in others. Second, its impact (i.e., whether the benefits outweigh the harm) depends both on children's individual needs and more important on how it is implemented by the school staff.

If this interpretation of the evidence is valid, then several conclusions seem in order:

1. Research effort should now go to examining the classroom process and to testing theoretically grounded propositions regarding factors in the school situation that affect its interracial climate.

2. Policy-makers should give more attention to balancing racial status within schools and less to balancing racial ratios between schools. Principals and teachers should be encouraged to experiment in ways of raising the status of the minority group.

3. The feasibility and advantage of stable, integrated neighborhoods as an alternative to intermetropolitan busing should be explored.

4. Children should not be assigned to schools solely on the basis of race; instead families should be given circumscribed

choice among schools that differ in educational philosophy as well as in location and racial ratio.

In drawing these conclusions as to policy I am admittedly on less sure ground than when reviewing the literature or reporting my own findings. The reader must believe that these ideas did not antedate or channel the empirical inquiry, but are my subsequent attempt to make sense out of all the evidence.

2. NEEDED RESEARCH

The 120 studies of school desegregation represent a tremendous investment in the form of federal and foundation funds and professional endeavor, an investment that in retrospect seems largely wasted. Not only have social theory and the principles of experimental design been largely ignored, there has also been much duplication that is not exact enough to serve as replication and that does not net data that can be pooled.

At this juncture further investigation of the broad question—Does desegregation benefit children?—would seem a poor use of national resources. The pressing need now is to discover the school conditions under which the benefits of mixed schooling are maximized and its hardships minimized. And to be worth the expenditure future inquiry must be coordinated, carefully designed, and guided by social and psychological theory.

The most needed type of research at this juncture is probably not a mammoth longitudinal testing program with measurements on dozens of background variables to allow exquisite statistical manipulation. True, if the right variables were measured and measured well the results might be very interesting. But far more illuminating would be small-scale studies involving anthropological observations of the process of interracial schooling, across settings diverse in black/white ratios and in middle-class/lower-class ratios, and also diverse in their educational philosophies and techniques. We need to learn more about the ways teachers think and do and how these affect the classroom climate. The conditions posited in Chapter 5 as essential to the type of desegregation that benefits children psychologically and that deserved the name integration can probably not be measured by questionnaire surveys, but they might be appraised by trained observers. The substudies would each ideally cover a number of years, with some system devised for summarizing a child's total classroom experience. For instance, he might be given a "cumulative classroom climate score" or an "average teacher fairness score," so that the correlation of racial experience and academic development over several years could be examined for a sample of children.

The narrow emphasis of most desegregation research on cognitive outcomes should also be expanded, and the still narrower emphasis on tests of verbal achievement standardized on a majority group population should be corrected. Ways of measuring many other potential outcomes of schooling—leadership, human sensitivity, understanding of one's cultural heritage, effective public speaking, and so forth—might be found. Racial conflict develops in many desegregated schools.[4] Does such conflict have positive or negative effects? Does it lead to growth of a healthy degree of militancy, political skill, self-confidence, or to the growth of unhealthy distrust, prejudice, and anomie?[5]

Researchers could make a further contribution to educational practice and social theory if they studied the interplay of individual characteristics and social context. What type of child flourishes in what type of setting? We should know.

Children in school today cannot benefit from the results of research released 10 years from now. But they may benefit if their school's policy is guided immediately by theoretically grounded hypotheses that will be tested scientifically over time. Variation in treatment is an essential ingredient of experimental design. When we are sure a particular treatment will save lives, giving a placebo to a control group is inhuman. There is no such certainty as the best means of achieving equality of status and good relations between pupils of different ethnic backgrounds. Instead, various educated guesses deserve a trial. While awaiting the results of research, then, school personnel need flexible guidelines and encouragement to innovate.

3. FROM DESEGREGATION TO INTEGRATION

As long as the dual school system prevailed in southern states and in many areas of the North, its elimination was necessarily the first order of business. Now, with that battle legally won and one-race schools everywhere eliminated or doomed, a new phase in the struggle for educational equality is beginning. In the years ahead, if children are to realize the promised benefits of desegregation, policy-makers and educators must give less attention to balancing schools and more attention to conditions within biracial schools. Unless schools are happy environments conducive to growth in competence, self-confidence, and mutual respect for minority group and majority group child alike, of what use is mathematically perfect racial distribution?

Considerations in Chapter 5 of the various social-psychological meanings of desegregation suggested a number of conditions that may facilitate the well-being of children in a biracial setting. The most important appear to be affirmative administrative leadership, recognition of the value of cultural pluralism, and equalization of group status.

At all levels, from the national adminstration to the local school, leadership may be the most essential variable in the achievement of integration. Many social scientists have flagged the importance of unequivocal commitment to the goal of integration on the part of superintendent, principal, and other sources of authority and of their firm public demonstration of the commitment.[6] Unfortunately, in the 1960s such leadership was lacking in community after community, and desegregation was usually achieved only as a result of federal or state action or court decision.[7]

Altshuler (1970) points out that "the history of efforts to combat segregation in America has been one of raising the level at which decisions were made" (p. 20). High-level decision-making facilitates change at the local level but may also undermine initiative and responsibility needed in policy implementation. Glazer (1972) considers it a serious drawback of many desegregation schemes that they greatly increase the power of high-level officials and central school bureaucracies. Since all school boards and school adminstrators do not accept integration as the goal, federal and state oversight must continue. But such oversight can take the form of example and examination of intent and results, rather than proscription of set formulas.

The selection and training of school staff for biracial schools appears all-important. The principal and his faculty have the responsibility for structuring the interracial climate of the school. Their nonracist attitudes, commitment to equality, justice, and democratic decision-making, their optimism as to the potential of the minority group child and determination to raise his achievement and aspiration set the stage for meaningful integration. Important too is firm protection of the rights of the minority and initiative and resourcefulness in finding ways to equalize status and resolve conflict.

An interracial faculty can help student-faculty communication as well as provide minority children with significant others of their own race. Giving minority group parents and other parents some voice in school affairs and the opportunity to serve in respected paraprofessional positions serves the same end. Teachers of all backgrounds who demonstrate respect for cultural diversity, who stress the contribution of minority groups to American life, and who make a place in the curriculum for study of African and Afro-American history, art, and literature probably reduce the minority group child's sense of cultural marginality or inferiority and the majority group child's ethno-centrism and feeling of superiority.

The hazards of desegregation for the black child stem in large part from the unequal status he may bring *to* the school and hence often is accorded *in* the school. As Rosenberg and Simmons (1971) demonstrate, racial isolation protects the lower-class black child from realizing his low social status, his low academic status, and his low racial status. Social class desegregation strips the first two defenses from him, while racial desegregation exposes him to awareness of prejudice against his race.

Though some resultant distress may be inevitable, much could be avoided by social engineering on the part of the staff. Avoidance of tracking, individualization of instruction, and provision of remedial help in a way that is not demeaning might reduce differentials in academic status. Important too would be giving black children opportunities to demonstrate publicly their competence in many ways besides athletics and of finding ways for black girls to earn social status comparable to that of their brothers who play on school teams.

For whites the hazard of simultaneously mixing children of different races and social class levels is that racial stereotypes and hostility will be augmented rather than diminished. Porter (1971), on the basis of her field observations with preschool children, concluded that differences in race and social class should not be allowed to reinforce each other. She advises encouraging SES heterogeneity within race but SES homogene-ity across race. But the demography of race and class being what it is in the 1970s, such a policy is not very promising. Lower-class whites are especially likely to be racist and have little know-how or academic motivation to share with lower-class blacks. Middle-class blacks are still too few to spread far and may not want to be scattered around as mission-aries to white suburbia. Instead, we urgently need educational experiments in ways of handling classroom heterogeneity in both race and class in ways that threaten neither the self-esteem of the minority group nor the racial attitudes of the majority group.

The achievement of racial democracy in a school cannot be legislated from outside. The best the central office can do is to select a staff that is strong, able, and committed to integration and then give them freedom to initiate and plenty of financial and technical assistance. In addition there should be provision for ombudsman or watchdog in the interest of the minority community and minority child.

4. METROPOLITAN OR NEIGHBORHOOD SCHOOLS?

Metropolitan consolidation is increasingly seen as the only solution to racial segregation in our cities. As long as the focus is on balancing ratios between schools this appears to be the inevitable direction in which legal, political, and educational thinking must move. But popular opposition is so intense that metropolitan desegregation of schools promises no peace on the racial front. Is residential desegregation a possible solution to the dilemma? Do integrated neighborhood schools have advantages over educational parks or cross-county exchanges?

The demography and politics of school desegregation have not been the major concern of this book and therefore cannot be adequately treated in a concluding chapter. But neither can the needs of children be faced without recognition of current demographic and political realities. Central cities continue to gain nonwhite and impoverished families and to lose to the suburbs white and upwardly mobile families. Racial and economic segregation in housing thus continues to increase. The decreasing quality of urban life, the incidence of crime, the threat of more riots, as well as overcrowding, teacher shortages, and racial conflict in city schools all contribute to the flight from the city of those who can afford to move, especially white families with school-aged children. With fear of further school desegregation, the rate accelerates.

National polls document increasing acceptance by white adults of desegregation in principle and for themselves in many areas of life, especially if association is limited to those of similar background and values. But there is continued and very strong white resistance to racial and social class desegregation in housing and in education, if that involves busing middle-class children to a lower-class neighborhood or accepting large numbers of lower-class children into middle-class schools. In fact, according to one survey, between March 1971, and March 1972 the percentage of Americans opposed to desegregation by busing in their community rose from 41 to 69.[8]

It is true that, on the surface, the South has at last accepted with extraordinary calm the demise of the dual school system. It is also true that many southern families who react by initially transferring their children to private schools eventually return to the desegregated public schools.[9] However, under seeming acceptance lies strong resistance to meaningful desegregation, that is, by busing. The percentage opposed in the Deep South was 87 in 1972.[10] Such attitudes influence voting behavior in national as well as local elections and will undoubtedly be translated eventually into "white flight" unless some factor in the equation changes.

In the North the desegregation issue polarizes community after community. In the 1960s, after a period of more or less intense pressure and jockeying, most school boards took affirmative steps toward desegregation (Holden, 1974).[11] According to Pettigrew's estimate (1969), roughly 30% of the population is segregationist at heart, 30% integrationist, and 40% moderates who swing according to the situation or times. In the 1960s the demands of civil rights groups focused on symbolic desegregation, that is, placing a few Negroes into white schools. To this most whites did not object strongly; by and large, moderates sided with liberals.[12]

But as the issue shifted to metropolitan desegregation with two-way busing of large numbers, white resistance mounted. The middle 40% of Americans swung to join the opposition. When racial mixing is not at issue, parents recognize that the neighborhood school is not sacred and that short-distance busing does not harm children. In fact, nearly 20 million pupils in the United States are currently being transported to school by buses at public expense for reasons other than desegregation.[13] But when the issue is racial desegregation, whites of all backgrounds become very defensive of the neighborhood school.

Rogers (1968) and Rubin (1972) have analyzed in detail the ambivalence in regard to full-scale school desegregation of otherwise liberal professional and middle-class citizens in New York City and in Richmond, California. Liberals' fear of loss of quality is greater than their espousal of equality in schooling. Working-class whites are more outspoken in their racial hostility and fierce defense of the neighborhood school. Their attitudes are interpreted by Rubin as due to rational fears as well as irrational prejudice. "Experience had taught them to suspect that there would be little benefit for their children in the proposed integration program" (p. 45). And "It is *their* jobs, *their* neighborhoods, *their* schools that are the most immediately threatened" (p. 66, emphasis added). Pettigrew (1971) found the same attitudes in Boston. Thus racial and social class bitterness reinforce each other. Unfortunately, polarization on the busing issue affects more than the course of desegregation. It may also overturn school boards or doom budget appropriations or bond issues, thus having grave effects on educational policy and quality.

Black opinion also is divided on the issue of mandatory desegregation by busing. The great majority of black adults favor desegregation—over 90% according to some polls.[14] They believe that a majority-white school is inevitably better equipped and better staffed than a majority-black school. Also, as Silberman (1964) has observed, they "have made school desegregation the touchstone of white sincerity and integrity'' (p. 292. To them it appears only fair that whites assume some of the burden involved—perhaps a long bus ride or an ancient school building. If a ghetto school is good enough for a black child, it is good enough for a white child, and his presence will insure equal treatment for that school. An antisegregation court decision is a victory for the whole black community.

But it does not follow that most black parents want their own children bused out of their neighborhood to a mostly white school.[15] Though usually convinced that only through desegregation can their children receive a high-quality education, nevertheless, according to the 1972 Harris poll, only 52% favor busing to achieve racial balance. As the black population of a city grows in numbers, political power, and militancy, its interest tends to shift from desegregation to adequate funding, accountability, and community control of its schools.[16] The closing of ghetto schools and mandatory out-busing of their pupils is viewed by many blacks as a way of perpetuating white supremacy.

Perhaps it is time to reconsider the possibility of residential desegregation in our metropolitan areas. In the 1960s a vigorous fair housing movement gained momentum, and legislation against discrimination was enacted in many states and cities.[17] If that movement were revitalized, if legislative loopholes were tightened and the discriminatory practices of real estate and banking firms were eliminated, it might be possible for housing to share with schools the responsibility of desegregating our society.

Hermalin and Farley (1973) find on the basis of 1970 census data that economic factors no longer adequately account for the concentration of blacks in central cities. An increasing black middle class can now afford suburban housing. Since recent opinion polls indicate that the majority of whites are willing to accept black neighbors or to have their children attend schools with black children,[18] these authors see residential integration as a means of achieving schools that are both integrated and neighborhood based.

The type of neighborhood that would contribute to the achievement of integrated schools and society would not be the familiar, racially changing, lower-class neighborhood on the edge of the black ghetto. As earlier chapters indicate, the benefits of desegregation have rarely been realized in such neighborhoods. Not a single sector but the whole suburban ring—stable working-class and middle-class areas alike—would have to be opened to racially mixed housing. As voluntary residents of integrated neighborhoods children would probably escape many of the threats of desegregation discussed above. They should be less stigmatized, feel less relative deprivation, and enjoy more equal status, and their parents could have more share in the control of the school than if they were bused in from a distance.[19]

In comparison with integrated neighborhood schools, mandatory, metropolitan-wide busing has many drawbacks. Not only does it incur the determined opposition of parents and expose children to potential social threat, but it also consumes scarce school funds and scarce gas and contributes to highway pollution and congestion. Involvement of working-class parents in school life is inevitably curtailed. Local sense of community may be destroyed and the power of the central bureaucracy increased. Though not inevitable, it is likely that metropolitan schools will be larger, more uniform, more impersonal than local schools, contributing further to the anomie of mass society.

This is not to suggest that voluntary exchange of pupils between city and suburban ring should be curtailed. On the contrary, such interchange should be vigorously promoted. But if enforced on a scale sufficient to desegregate the largest metropolitan areas, two-way busing might have social costs that would outweigh its benefits.

5. SCHOOL ASSIGNMENT POLICY

The importance of the actor's perception and definition of the situation runs through the analysis in the previous chapter of the meanings of desegregation. Symbolic message, stigma, relative deprivation, expectation, normative or comparative reference group, marginality, social or academic threat, status among peers—all must be perceived in order to be felt. A free individual will choose a situation he expects to find (on balance) favorable. Conversely, a situation that has been freely chosen tends to be perceived as favorable. Thus voluntary desegregation may have assets that mandatory desegregation lacks.

Moreover, whatever the effect of social class mixture, racial ratios, community control, and other conditions in the school on children *in general,* individual differences, child to child, make it unlikely that any one treatment is equally good for all. Misfits might be reduced if families were allowed some choice (not unlimited choice) between schools of various educational philosophies, of various social and racial clienteles, and at various distances from home.

Parental choice among schools is in disrepute because it has so often been used as an evasive device by school boards attempting to avoid meaningful desegregation. To stay court-ordered desegregation or to counter pressure from civil rights groups, many southern communities gave black parents the right to transfer their children to formerly all-white schools. Other communities (more often in the North) allowed open enrollment in any school in which there were empty seats. It is obvious from an examination of the record that most of these schemes were either designed to allow white parents to avoid any racial mixing for their children or else were implemented by reluctant adminstrators in a way that resulted in little desegregation for black children.[20] Thus the potentials of parental or pupil choice in achieving a large measure of desegregation have been neither fully explored nor disproven. Two ingredients seem to have been missing: commitment to maximum integration on the part of school boards and administrators and restriction against "white flight." Freedom to choose and the rights of the majority must, as always in a democracy, be within limits. If whites are allowed to elect all-white schools, the rights of blacks who prefer integration will be curtailed. It thus seems both necessary and justifiable to deny to whites the right to transfer out of a school which blacks choose to enter, and at the same time to set a very broad quota on the number of non-neighborhood children allowed to transfer to a school (49%?).

Neighborhoods can also be defined to be as racially inclusive as possible by redrawing district lines or by pairing schools within walking distance of each other. Such redistricting may cost less, arouse less resentment, and stigmatize children less than crosstown busing.[21]

There are also more controversial questions: Should families be allowed to refuse assignment to a school that is very distant or in a totally different neighborhood? Should a child be allowed to transfer out of a school in which classmates are *predominantly* of the other race, even if such a transfer does not promote racial balance? I am not sure what the answer to these questions should be but tend to feel that such refusals and transfers should be allowed. If they are not, resentment will build and the child may be placed under a psychological burden, which will fall disproportionately—as burdens usually do—on the poor and politically weak. Middle-class parents of any ethnic group will find a way to get their children into the schools of their choice.

Some argue that mandatory pupil assignment is necessary to dismantle a dual school system, North or South. In most communities this may be true. In others the removal of barriers to freedom and the encouragement of choice within limits might accomplish the same purpose with less friction.[22] If most black parents prefer integrated schools (and polls frequently find that they do), and if they are given free transportation and encouraged to use up to 49% of available spaces in the schools they prefer, and if white children are not allowed to transfer out, then except in those few cities with huge ghettoes, a large measure of desegregation could be achieved with a minimum of mandatory assignment.[23] In cities less than 50% black it would be logistically (though perhaps not financially) possible, through the addition of temporary classrooms or new schools in areas which families prefer, to allow every black family a choice between a "balanced" or a majority-own-group neighborhood school. If black families in these cities choose racially mixed schools, white neighborhood schools would be balanced. The one option that cannot be open is for whites to transfer away from schools as black children transfer in.

In cities over half black, if large numbers of blacks wanted integration, then black applicants for majority-white schools would have to be bused to the suburbs or selected by lot to maintain some majority-white (51%+) schools. Implementing these principles would probably slow the flight of whites and maintain a higher degree of integration than an open-door policy which allowed every school to become majority black.

Some black families may prefer first-rate neighborhood or majority-black schools for their children. If these majority-black schools are of high quality and educationally interesting, they may be chosen by some white families as well. Maybe courts will allow that option, provided the option of a balanced school is also readily available for every child. The closing of black schools seriously affects black personnel, can be an insult to the black community, and can leave it without a much-needed resource and focus for neighborhood organization. Entin (1972) suggests that the desegregation plan lately adopted in Jacksonville, Florida, follows a model that is increasingly common in the South. Systemwide, sweeping desegregation was there accomplished through closing eight black schools but no white schools. Black students are in the minority in 125 out of 129 schools and ride the bus for 10 years, whereas white students are bused to central city schools only for the sixth and seventh grades. Such a plan, Entin suggests, makes black students assume a disproportionate share of the burden of desegregation and "clearly imparts the psychological message of the inferiority of black institutions and personnel" (p. 11).

A more equitable model is provided by Goldsboro, North Carolina.[24] There black and white faculty were reshuffled throughout the system, ghetto schools were maintained and improved, and the amount of cross-city busing divided proportionately between black and white pupils. But, though more equitable, the Goldsboro system gives families no choice and probably leaves many on both sides of town unhappy with the arrangement. Each local situation is in some respects unique. Mandatory crosstown busing may be a necessary interim measure in communities such as Goldsboro and Jacksonville. In others some measure of choice within well-defined limits can be incorporated into desegregation schemes.[25]

School officials will have to promote open enrollment vigorously if they hope to offset the prejudices and inertia of parents who are wedded to their neighborhood schools. Publicity, encouragement, home visits, counseling, the provision of new buses with convenient schedules, and new educational programs are among the affirmative techniques that might be employed to persuade as many parents as possible to transfer their children to biracial schools. Another device is to assign students to a biracial school but allow transfers out by petition, rather than the opposite policy of assignment to a neighborhood school and allowing desegregation by petition. Desegregating whole classrooms together as in Hartford or neighborhood blocks as in Berkeley capitalizes on group morale and reduces refusals.[26]

An imaginative plan for Springfield, Massachusetts, includes not only allowing families first, second, and third choices among schools in their quadrant of the city and a lottery whenever racial quotas cannot be met voluntarily, but also such variation in educational program, school to school, as is calculated to attract middle-class families to central city schools and ghetto families to schools on the periphery of the city.[27]

Building choice into the desegregation plans need not mean the postponement of integration for another generation, or allowing blacks to be intimidated and whites to avoid racially mixed schools, or embarking on a weak middle-of-the-road policy. It does mean taking the following into account:

1. The psychological power of self-determination.
2. The potential harm of conscription of all kinds and of school assignment in disregard of the diverse needs of individual children.
3. The danger of forcing the most hostile into a situation they resent.

Americans are nearly unanimously in favor of the nation remaining one society under one Constitution, not two societies—one black, one white. Almost everybody agrees that legal segregation is morally wrong, and a good majority of citizens also believe that integration should be the goal in all areas of public life, including school. Judicial interpretation of the Constitutional mandate for the elimination of dual school systems, North and South, has expanded steadily. What we need now is to discover not whether school integration is a fine objective, but which are the best ways of implementing it.

During the past 20 years considerable racial mixing has taken place in schools, but research has produced little evidence of dramatic gains for children and some evidence of genuine stress for them. The probable reason for such outcomes is that desegregation is rarely true integration; in other words, it is rarely implemented in ways that give minority children equal status and full protection against victimization and cultural marginality.

Some believe that what it accomplishes for society and race relations in general is the most important aspect of desegregation. Thus Jencks (1972b) suggests that we should not evaluate busing primarily in terms of what happens to the children on the buses, but whether it contributes to further social and economic justice for blacks. This reasoning seems to me a half-truth, for I would also argue that the welfare of a generation of children cannot be ignored with impunity and that minimizing the harm and maximizing the benefits of desegregation will contribute substantially to black progress.

What is needed now is a period of vigorous experimentation in ways of achieving equality of educational opportunity. School boards, principals, and teachers must have the freedom to examine alternatives in all aspects of schooling, not merely ethnic ratios. But we cannot afford infinite variation, aimless experimentation, or limitless choice. The boundaries must be set through continued public acknowledgment that integration is the goal and through federal and state monitoring as schools search for appropriate means of realizing it. And while schoolmen are learning ways of translating desegregation into integration, wise public policy, I believe, will allow parents and children, also, maximum choice among permissable educational alternatives.

NOTES

1. Parts 3, 4, and 5 of this chapter are a much revised version of a paper published in *Integrated Education* in 1972. (See Bibliography.)
2. Office of Civil Rights (1971), Rossell and Crain (1973)
3. Greeley and Sheatsley (1971).
4. Dorr (1972).
5. Cf. Pettigrew (1971), pp. 97-98.
6. Dean and Rosen (1955); Yarrow and Yarrow (1958); Dentler (1966).
7. Hill and Feeley (1967); Mack (1968).
8. Harris (1972); see also Zimmer and Hawley (1968).
9. Palmer (1971).
10. Harris (1972); see also Tumin (1958).
11. Hill and Feeley (1967); Mack (1968); Kirby (1970), Holden (1974).
12. Crain (1968).
13. MARC (1972).

14.   Marx (1967); Campbell and Schuman (1968). Goldman (1970), in *A Report from Black America*, shows that the attitudes of blacks toward busing varies with the region, age, and sex of the respondent. In answer to the question, "Would you like to see children in your family be picked up in buses every day to go to school with white children in some other part of town?," older, low-income, or southern respondents were more affirmative (p. 268).

15.   The National Black Political Convention meeting in Gary, Indiana, in the spring of 1972 passed resolutions opposing both segregated schools and busing for racial balance. "We condemn racial integration of schools as a notion that black children are unable to learn unless they are in the same setting as white children. As an alternative to busing of black children to achieve racial balance, we demand quality education in the black community by controlling of our school districts and a guarantee of an equal share of the money." As quoted by Miriam Wasserman, in "Busing as a 'Cover Issue' — A Radical View," *The Urban Review*, 6:1 (September-October, 1972), 6-10. However, on May 19 the convention released guidelines to be used for black political activity which said in part: "Busing is not the real issue in American education today, and we condemn the dishonesty of the Nixon Administration and other forces in making busing an issue when, in fact, busing has officially been used to maintain segregation for many years in many sections of the country. The real education issue for the black community is how do we get supreme quality education for all our youngsters" (*The New York Times*, 20 May 1972). See Charles V. Hamilton, *The New York Times Magazine*, 1 October 1972 ("The Nationalist vs. the Integrationist") for an enlightening essay on the painful division of opinion that white resistance to desegregation has engendered within the black community.

16.   See Altshuler (1970) on the feasibility and merit of black control of black institutions, including schools.

17.   Saltman (1972).

18.   However, Anthony Downs (1968) develops what he calls the "Law of Dominance": "A vast majority of whites of all income groups would be willing to send their children to integrated schools or live in integrated neighborhoods, as long as they were sure that the white group concerned would remain in the majority in those facilities or areas" (p. 1338). See also the National Academy of Science (1972).

19.   Strickman (1972) suggests that community should be defined not in terms of race or neighborhood but in terms of the parents, teachers, and students of a given school. Metropolitan consolidation, together with

decentralization, could give the school's community so defined, and black parents as part of that community, more say in educational policy than they have at present.

20. U.S. Commission on Civil Rights (1966, 1967); Weinberg (1967); Dimond (1971); Rogers (1968).

21. Jencks et al. (1972) argue for complete freedom of choice in public assignment and suggest that a "public" school should by definition be one that is open to any student who wants to attend.

22. See Alexander Bickel (1970) and Center for the Study of Public Policy (1970) for a discussion of legal barriers to freedom of choice in schools. Professor Bickel does not believe that federal courts must necessarily interpret such choice as unconstitutional even where it results in some racial imbalance. A reversal of legal support for assimilation as the duty of public schools is also possible.

23. See Goodman (1972) for a description of a northern community (Green-burgh, New York—one-third black), where mandatory crosstown busing for everyone has gone on for 20 years, to the apparent satisfaction of most citizens.

24. King and Mayer (1971).

25. Havighurst (1972) urges that school systems find ways to maximize options and flexibility. "Busing to achieve racial integration in a school is often desirable, but there probably should be an option which permits every student to attend the school nearest his home if he wishes to do so" (p. 309).

26. Mahan (1968); Sullivan (1969).

27. Clinchy (1972).

Appendix

Chart A-1. Cross-sectional studies of black achievement (comparison of experimental and control groups, but no pretest)

Study	Place	N Integrated/ Segregated	Grade Level	Design How Dese-gregated?	Comparison	Controls	Pretest/ Posttest[a]	Outcomes for Desegregated IQ or Verbal	Read-ing	Math	General or Unspecified	Remarks
Boland (1968)	Five major Connecticut cities	All pupils in 47 elem. schools; 1/3 seniors in 13 H.S.	6 12	Neighborhood	School % black	Father's education and occupation	None/HN[a]	0				No significance tests. No difference on Henmon Nelson IQ by school % black
Crowley (1932)	Cincinnati, O.	55/55	4-6	Neighborhood	4 mixed versus 2 segregated schools	IQ, age (SES was equivalent)	None/	0	0	0	0	No significant difference on 11 out of 13 tests
Jessup (1967)	New York City	18/80 Black and Puerto Rican	2,5	Neighborhood	1 mixed versus 2 segregated schools	Neighborhood SES, school facilities, ethnicity	None/				+	Children from low SES neighborhood score significantly higher in desegregated school on standardized achievement tests
Lockwood (1966)	An upstate New York city	90/127	6	Neighborhood	Pupils in 5 balanced schools (2+ yr.) versus pupils in 2 imbalanced schools (2+ yr.)	IQ, not SES (SES of balanced school was higher)	None/ITBS				+	Pupils in balanced schools score significantly higher at all IQ levels, but the difference tends to disappear for those in balanced schools for less than 2 years
Long (1968)	Northern suburb	45/53	K-2	Neighborhood	1 mixed versus 1 segregated school	IQ, SES	None/MAT				0	No significant difference in achievement with IQ and SES controlled

Study	Location	N	Grade	School race measure	Comparison	Controls	Test	Results	Comments
Matzen (1965)	San Francisco Bay Area	1100 in 11 schools	5,7	Neighborhood	Classroom % black	IQ, SES	None/CAT		Classroom % black tends to be negatively related to achievement, but (esp. at grade 7) may be due to homogenous grouping
Robertson (1967)	Pontiac, Mich.	120	10	Neighborhood	Average B/W ratio in J.H.S.	IQ	None/CSS	0, +	No significant difference in achievement with IQ controlled, but GPA is higher for graduates of integrated junior high schools
Samuels (1958)	New Albany, Ind.	45/45	1-6	Neighborhood	2 mixed schools versus 2 segregated schools	IQ, SES, health, Preschool readiness, attendance	None/MAT	−, +, −, +	Higher achievement scores for segregated in gr. 1 and 2; higher achievement scores for mixed in gr. 3-6
Wilson (1961)	Berkeley, Calif	19/73	6	Neighborhood	Schools 14% black versus 62% black	No	None/CAT	+, +, −	No significance tests. Achievement scores tend to be higher, but teacher evaluation tends to be lower in schools 14% black

Cross-sectional Studies with Longitudinal Measure of School Race

Study	Location	N	Grade	School race measure	Comparison	Controls	Test	Results	Comments
Johnson et al. (1967)	Chicago, Ill.	121	College freshmen	Neighborhood	School % white Grades 9-12	No	None/GPA	+	No significance tests. GPA for graduates of seg. high school = 2.45; GPA for graduates of mixed high school = 2.78

Chart A-1. Cross-sectional studies of black achievement (comparison of experimental and control groups, but no pretest) (Concl.)

Study	Place	N Integrated/ Segregated	Grade Levels	How Desegregated?	Comparison	Controls	Pretest/ Posttest[a]	IQ or Verbal	Reading	Math	General or Unspecified	Remarks
St. John (1962)	New Haven, Conn.	230	10-11	Neighborhood	School % white Grades 1-9	Sex, SES, IQ, birthplace	None/DA	0 +	0	0	0	Significantly higher verbal apt. for those desegregated early; no significant difference on IQ, reading, or GPA
St. John (1973)	Pittsburgh, Pa.	984	8	Neighborhood	School % white Grades 1-8	Sex, SES, School SES (1-8)	None/MAT	0	0	+	+ 0	Significant positive relation between school % white and achievement in language and arithmetic, not reading or science
Wolff (1963)	Plainfield, N.J.	20/39	12	Neighborhood	School % white elem. grades	No	None/ND				+	No significance tests. Higher GPA for those desegregated early. Quantitative aptitude, or Nelson Denny Reading grade level tends to favor desegregation

[a] See chart A-4 for Key.

Chart A-2. Longitudinal studies of black achievement (comparison of pre-measures and postmeasures, but no control group)

| | | N | | Design | | | | Outcomes for Desegregated | | | | |
| | | | | | | | | IQ or | Read- | | General or | |
Study	Place	Integrated/ Segregated	Grade Level	How Desegregated?	Comparison	Controls	Pretest/ Posttest[a]	Verbal	ing	Math	Unspecified	Remarks
Archibald (1967)	METCO Boston, Mass.	64	3-8	Voluntary busing to suburbs	1 year gain versus National Norms	No	MAT/MAT		+	0	+	Significant gain in word knowledge, reading, and spelling, but not in arithmetic
Bryant (1968)	Angleton. Tex.	139	8-11	Segregated school closed	1year gain postdesegregation	Sex	STAP/STAP				−	The mean gains in achievement test scores and in GPA were significantly less than the expected norm
Dambacher (1971)	Berkeley, Cal.	All blacks in city, over 2800	1-6	Total district; busing- B:K-3, W:4-6	2-year gain; post-versus predesegregation	No	CPT/CPT SAT/SAT		0			No significance tests. On the SAT and CPT Reading, the trends do not favor the desegregated.[b]
Graves and Bedell (1967)	White Plains, N.Y.	33/36	3-6	Redistricting via busing and walking	3-year gain versus gain of former segregated	No	SAT/SAT		+ − 0	+ − 0		Overall, there was somewhat less of a decline on the SAT relative to national norms for the desegregated than for blacks in earlier segregated schools

Chart A-2. Longitudinal studies of black achievement (comparison of pre-measures and post-measures, but no control group) (Contd.)

Study	Place	N Integrated/ Segregated	Grade Levels	How Desegregated?	Comparison	Controls	Pretest/ Posttest[a]	IQ or Verbal	Reading	Math	General or Unspecified	Remarks
Hansen (1960)	Washington, D.C.	All blacks in city	3,5,6 8,9	Dual system eliminated; imbalance remains	4-year gain; post- versus predesegregation	No	ITBS/ITBS PAT/PAT CAT/CAT				+	No significance tests. Different criterion tests were used. General rise in achievement, even in segregated schools
Hsia (1971)	Evanston, Ill.	All blacks in city, c. 1000	1,3,4,8	Redistricting via busing and walking	3-year gain versus national norms	No (bused lower SES than walkers)	CPT/CPT STEP/STEP		0	+		No consistent significant gains. Bused gain significantly more often than walkers; formerly integrated black girls gain more than formerly segregated
Katzenmeyer (1962)	Jackson, Mich.	All blacks in city: 193	K-2	Neighborhood	2-year gain: blacks versus whites	No	LT/LT	+				Mean IQ gain of blacks = 6.68, of whites = 1.87; black gain unrelated to school % white (1-6)
Marcum (1968)	Urbana, Ill.	160	3-6	Total district; pupil transfer from 1 segregated to 8 other schools	1-year gain: post- versus predesegregation	No	CAT/CAT				0	No significance tests reported. Little, if any, gain in achievement. Decreasing growth rate both pre- and postdesegregation

Design: How Desegregated?, Comparison, Controls, Pretest/Posttest[a]

Outcomes for Desegregated: IQ or Verbal, Reading, Math, General or Unspecified

Study	Location / Sample	N	Grades	Desegregation	Comparison	Controls	Tests				Findings
Mayer et al. (1973)	Goldsboro, N. Carolina	232	3-5	Total system reassignment	Gain versus national norms	None	SAT/SAT	+	+	+	Significant gain from grade 3 to 5 relative to national norms (gain = 4.3 verbal and 2.9 math in standardized scores). Black/white gap not significantly reduced
Maynor (1970)	Hoke County, N. Carolina	680	6-12	Total district	1-year gain: post versus pre-desegration race	IQ teacher's race	CAT/CAT	+	+	+	Blacks show significantly higher language and math scores after desegregation, regardless of teacher's race
McCullough (1972)	Goldsboro, N. Carolina	Entire class, c. 4000	7,8,9,11 cohort	Total district	2-year gain post-desegregation	No	SAT/SAT		+	+	Significant gain in reading (esp. for upper quartile); the predesegregation downward trend in math is arrested
Perry (1973)	National ABC Program	619	12	Selective boarding	2- to 4-year gain postdesegregation	No	SSAT/SAT	0			No significant difference in test scores
Prichard (1969)	Chapel Hill, N. Carolina	180/90	5,7,9	Total system	1-year gain predesgregation (versus) 1 and 2-year gain postdesegregation	No	STEP/STEP	0	+ / 0	0	Significant gain in math for grades 5 and 7, not for 9; No significant change in reading for any grade
Purl and Dawson (1973)	Riverside, Cal.	All blacks and Chicanos in city (225+)	K-3	Total district; 3 segregated schools closed, 1/3 pupils bused	Mean achievement relative to national norms, 1965-1972	Sex, grade, ethnicity	MRT/MRT SAT/SAT CPT/CPT	0	0	–	Achievement of K-1 rose steadily and significantly; achievement of grade 2 showed no trend; achievement of grade 3 decreased slightly

Chart A-2. Longitudinal studies of black achievement (comparison of pre-measures and post-measures, but no control group) (Concl.)

Study	Place	N Integrated/ Segregated	Design				Outcomes for Desegregated					Remarks
			Grade Levels	How Desegregated?	Comparison	Controls	Pretest/ Posttest [a]	IQ or Verbal	Read- ing	Math	General or Unspecified	
Stallings (1959)	Louisville, Ky.	All blacks in city: 2647/2897	2, 6, 8	Dual system eliminated: Imbalance remains	Predesegregation versus 14-month to 2-year gain post-desegregation	No	CAT/CAT SAT/SAT				+	Significant gains for integrated blacks; gains were greater for blacks who chose to remain with black teahcers (i.e., probably in segregated schools)

[a] See chart A-4 for key.

[b] Dambacher's (1971) findings are hard to interpret since different tests were used pre and post and since services were reduced following desegreagtion (Frelow, 1971).

Chart A-3. Quasi-experimental studies of black achievement (four-celled, comparison of premeasures and postmeasures for experimental and control group)

| | | N | | | Design | | | | Outcomes for Desegregated | | | | |
| | | Integrated/ | Grade | How Dese- | | | Pretest/ | IQ or | Read- | | | General or | |
Study	Place	Segregated	Level	gregated?	Comparison	Controls	Posttest[a]	Verbal	ing	Math		Unspecified	Remarks
Anderson (1966)	Nashville, Tenn.	75/75	4-6	School Redistricting	2-year gain versus nontransfer	Age, IQ, sex, intact family neighborhood, SES	Equivalent grade 2 ach/MAT	+				+	IQ and MAT achievement significantly higher in desegregated schools. The younger the age at which desegregation occurs, the greater the benefit
Armor (1972a)	METCO Boston, Mass.	195/41 147/41	7-12 elem.	Voluntary busing to suburbs	7-month gain versus nontransfer siblings	Family, sex, grade level	MAT/MAT		0 0	0 0		—	No significant difference in gains at either level on either reading or arithmetic; GPA for the desegregated in grades 7-12 declined significantly[b]
Banks and DiPasquale (1969)	Buffalo, N.Y.	1200/?	5-7	Selected pupils bused to 22 schools within city	1-year gain versus nontransfer	No	SAT/SAT		+				No significance tests reported. There was a 2½-month gain for the desegregated on the SAT paragraph meaning test
Beker (1967)	Syracuse, N.Y.	60/?	1-3	Voluntary transfer within city	1-year gain versus nontransfer	IQ	MRT/MRT SAT/SAT		+			+ 0	Significant gain on MRT for grade 1; no significant gain on SAT for gr. 2 and 3, but a positive trend in grade 3

?>
Chart A-3. Quasi-experimental studies of black achievement (four-celled, comparison of premeasures and postmeasures for experimental and control group) (Contd.)

Study	Place	N Integrated/Segregated	Grade Level	How Desegregated?	Comparison	Controls	Pretest/Posttest[a]	IQ or Verbal	Reading	Math	General or Unspecified	Remarks
Carrigan (1969)	Ann Arbor, Mich.	162/350 Same	K-5	Total district busing and walking from closed school	1-year gain versus nontransfer in school 48% black	No (2 groups differed in SES and initial scores)	LT/LT GRT/GRT LCRT/LCRT CAT/CAT	0 +	0	0	0	Few significant differences, but transfer pupils tend to have smaller gains; there was a rise in IQ for the kindergarten pupils
	Aberdeen's subsample ¼ original transfer group			Ditto	3-year gain	Ditto	Ditto	0				Initial gap in reading achievement between transfer and receiving pupils still present after 3 years of desegregation
Clinton (1969)	"Project Concern," New Haven, Conn.	109/106	2,3	Voluntary busing to suburbs	5-month gain versus non-bused	Age, sex, random assignment	CAT/CAT		+ 0	+ 0	0 0	Bused made significant gains in reading and math, not language, and for grade 2 only, not grade 3 on any test
Danahy (1971)	Minneapolis, Minn.	41/41	2-6	Voluntary busing within city	1-year gain versus nontransfer	No	GRT/GRT		+			No significant difference in achievement gains but the gains of the transfer pupils were greater than those of the nontransfer
Denmark and Guttentag (1969)	N.Y. suburb	15/48	Preschool	1 desegregated versus 3 segregated programs	2- to 8-month gain: desegregated versus segregated	All low SES	RPT/RPT LIPS/LIPS				0	No significant difference in cognitive growth between children in desegregated and segregated programs

Study	Location	N	Grade(s)	Description	Comparison	Controls	Test				Comments
Dressler (1967)	Buffalo, N.Y.	54/60	3	Pupils transfer from imbalanced to 12 balanced schools	1-year gain versus nontransfer	No	SAT/SAT		+		No significance tests reported. "Much greater gains" for desegregated in reading subtest of SAT
Evans (1969)	Texas	99/99	4-6	Total district	8-month gain versus segregated	IQ, sex, ESS, grade, class % black (25%/50%/75%)	ITBS/ITBS			− +	No significant gain on ITBS. Integrated girls gained "much less" than segregated girls and integrated boys slightly more than segregated boys. Among integrated, those with lower IQ, in class with higher % black, and boys gained more
Fortenberry (1959)	Oklahoma City	57/124 (57 = N reading test)	8-9	Desegregated versus segregated neighborhood	2-year gain versus segregated	IQ, sex	CAT/CAT	+	−	+	Desegregated made greater gains (not significant) in language and arithmetic, but less gain (not significant) in reading
Fox (1966, 1967, 1968)	New York City	941/?	3-6	Open enrollment with transportation	3-year gain versus nontransfer	No	MAT/MAT		0		No significance tests reported. No difference between open enrollment and controls in achievement
Frary and Goolsby (1970)	Gulfport, Miss.	26/81	1	School district experimental project	1-year gain: 9 desegregated versus 11 segregated classes	SES, IQ	MRT/MAT			+ 0	Low readiness, integrated pupils scored significantly higher; no significant difference for the medium readiness pupils
Gardner et al. (1970)	Chicago, Ill.	126/128	6-8	Voluntary busing parochial pupils to suburbs	2-year gain versus nontransfer	No			0	0	No significant difference in either grades or test performance between bused and nonbused blacks when adjustments are made for internal difference in achievement level

Chart A-3. Quasi-experimental studies of black achievement (four-celled, comparison of premeasures and postmeasures for experimental and control group) (Contd.)

Study	Place	N Integrated/ Segregated	Design					Outcomes for Desegregated				Remarks
			Grade Level	How Desegregated?	Comparison	Controls	Pretest/ Posttest[a]	IQ or Verbal	Reading	Math	General or Unspecified	
Griffin (1969)	Tulsa, Okla.	32/32	4-6	Redistricting	1-year gain: desegregated versus segregated	Matched on IQ, sex, SES, age	KA/KA SAT/SAT	+	+			Desegregated made significantly greater gains on the Kuhlman-Anderson and Stanford Achievement Tests
Heller et al. (1972)	Westport, Conn.	25/28	1-3	Voluntary busing to suburbs	1-year gain versus nontransfer	No	MAT/MAT				+	No significance tests. Trends favor the desegregated
Jonsson (1967); Sullivan (1968)	Berkeley, Cal.	250/?	1-6	Selected pupils bused to "Hills"	1-year gain versus nontransfer	No	SAT/SAT		+			No significance tests reported. Bused pupils made higher gains in reading
Klein (1967)	A southern city	38/38	10	Voluntary transfer	1-year gain: integrated versus segregated	Age, SES, Sex, aspiration, family size	CPT/CPT				0	No significant difference in English, biology, arithmetic, algebra, or geometry
Laird and Weeks	Philadelphia, Pa.	99/420	4-6	Voluntary busing	1-year gain versus nontransfer	IQ, Sex, grade			+ 0	0		Bused performed better than expected on basis of IQ at grades

152

Study	Ratio	Grade	Program	Comparison	Controls	Test	Effect	Results
(1966)								4-5 in reading (significant) and grades 5-6 in math (not significant)
Laurent (1969)	40/40	elem. J.H.S.	program in city Neighborhood	3-year gain: nonsegregated versus segregated	IQ, SES, age, grade	STEP/STEP ITBS/ITBS	0	No significant effect for school racial composition at grades 1-6 (STEP) or junior high (ITBS)
Mahan (1968)	197/244	K-5	Random classes bused to suburbs	2-year gain versus nontransfer	No (but random classes)	WISC/WISC PMA/PMA MRT/MRT ITBS/STEP	+ + − −	K-3: significant IQ gain for transfer, 4-5: significant IQ gain for nontransfer; K and 3: significant achievement gain for transfer. 4 and 5: significant achievement gain for nontransfer
Mayer et al. (1973)	20/122/72	3-5	Total system reassignment	2-year gain: much versus some versus no desegregation experience	Open/traditional teacher; neighborhood SES	SAT/SAT	0 +	Verbal: significant gain for all groups; no significant difference between groups in gain; math: significantly greater gain for desegregated than for segregated
Moorefield (1967)	82/258	4,6	Busing to schools with varying degree of integration	1-year gain: transfer versus nontransfer	No (desegregated) school of higher SES	ITBS/ITBS	0	No significant difference in reading achievement gain; trend for transferred boys to do less well than nontransferred boys
Rentsch (1967)	70/70	K-5	Open enrollment	1-year gain versus nontransfer	Matched on sex, achievement, GPA, attendance	SRA/SRA	0	No significant difference in reading

Chart A-3. *Quasi-experimental studies of black achievement (four-celled, comparison of premeasures and postmeasures for experimental and control group) (Contd.)*

Study	Place	Integrated/ Segregated (N)	Grade Levels	How Desegregated?	Comparison	Controls	Pretest/ Posttest [a]	IQ or Verbal	Reading	Math	General or Unspecified	Remarks
			Design					Outcomes for Desegregated				
Rochester School Board (1970)	Rochester, N.Y.	All pupils in certain classes and schools (in most cases, N < 50.)	3-6	Busing within city	2- to 3-year gain: desegregated & bused/desegregated inner city/segregated & compensatory/ segregated and noncompensatory	No (higher prescore for desegregated on many tests)	NYAT/NYAT ITBS/ITBS		+ − 0	+ − 0		Trends favor the desegregated but few of the tests are significant; higher gains for those integrated in K-3 than for those integrated in 4-6
Rock et al. (1968)	Rochester to W. Irondequoit, N.Y.	59/40	K-2	Voluntary busing to suburbs	3-year gain versus nontransfer	Teacher's rating of initial ability	MAT/MAT	+ 0	+ 0	+ 0		Bused pupils showed significant gains on 13 out of 27 tests
Sacramento Board of Ed. (1971)	Sacramento, Cal.	1600 Negro and Mexican Americans	2-6	Redistricting by busing within city	8-month gain: desegregated versus segregated	Matched on Sex, age, IQ, and ethnic group	CAT/CAT		+ 0	+ 0		Desegregated showed significantly greater gains in reading only in grade 4 and in math only in grade 4 and 6; other differences were positive and approached significance
St. John and Lewis	Boston, Mass.	412	6	Neighborhood, open enroll-	School % white grades 1-6	Sex, SES, school SES,	MAT/MAT	0	0	+	0	Significant positive relation with school % white on arithmetic

Study	Sample	Grades	Type of desegregation	Design	Controls	Tests			Comments
(1971) and Lewis and St. John (1974)			ment, and some busing	grades 1-6					achievement, not reading, IQ, or GPA
Samuels (1971)	"Project Concern," New Haven, Conn. 37/51/50	2	Voluntary busing to suburbs	2-year gain: desegregated versus segregated or compensatory	Random assignment, age, sex, reading aptitude	MAT/MAT SAT/SAT	+	0	Desegregated showed significantly greater gain than segregated or compensatory groups in reading, not math
School Board (1972)	Shaker Heights, O. 140/?	4-6	Voluntary transfer within city	7-month gain versus nontransfer	No	SAT/SAT	0	—	No significance tests reported. Grade 4: no difference in achievement; grade 5-6: less gain in achievement for desegregated
Slone (1968)	New York City 32/80	4	Paired schools	1-year gain: desegregated versus segregated	Matched on IQ, reading achievement, SES	MAT/MAT ITBS/ITBS	0	+	Desegregated showed significantly greater gain in math and almost significant gain in other subjects
Walberg (1969)	METCO Boston, Mass. 737/352	2-12	Voluntary busing to suburbs	47% of bused versus 27% of siblings	Home background	MAT/MAT	0	+	Desegregated showed significant gains in math only, grades 5 and 6
Williams (1968)	Brevard Co., Fla. 29/42	12	Voluntary transfer	3-year gain versus nontransfer	Desegregated slightly higher in SES		0	+	Desegregated scored significantly higher on 5 out of 6 Florida statewide tests

Chart A-3. *Quasi-experimental studies of black achievement (four-celled, comparison of premeasures and postmeasures for experimental and control group) (Concl.)*

Study	Place	N Integrated/ Segregated	Design Grade Levels	Design How Desegregated?	Comparison	Controls	Pretest/ Posttest[a]	Outcomes for Desegregated IQ or Verbal	Reading	Math	General or Unspecified	Remarks
Wilson (1967)	San Francisco Bay Area	905	6,8,11	Neighborhood	Relation: early school % white and later test scores	IQ, SES, school SES	SAT/SAT DAT/DAT		0			No significant effect for school race, with school SES and family SES controlled, in SAT, grade 6, or DAT, grades 8 and 11
Wolman (1964)	New Rochelle, N.Y.	½ pupils in segregated school	K-5	Voluntary busing within district	1-year gain versus nontransfer	No	MAT/MAT		+ 0			Desegrated in kindergarten only showed significantly greater gains
Wood (1969)	"Project Concern," Hartford, Conn.	266/303	K-5	Voluntary busing to suburbs	1-year gain: bused versus segregated	Matched on IQ	WISC/WISC	+ 0				Deseregated in K-1 and 2-3 gained significantly in IQ and desegregated girls in grades 4-5 gained significantly in IQ
Zdep and Joyce (1969)	Newark and Verona, N.J.	26/29	1,2	Voluntary busing to suburbs	1-year gain versus nontransfer	No	MRT/CPT CPT/CPT				+	Desegregated showed significant gain at both grade levels in achievement

[a] See Chart A-4 for key.

[b] Dambacher's (1971) findings are hard to interpret since different tests were used *pre and* post and since services were reduced following desegregation (Frelow, 1971).

[c] Armor's (1972a) study is much weakened by high nonresponse rate, especially for control group of siblings. See Pettigrew et al. (1973) for a careful critique of this study.

Chart A-4. Studies of white achievement (all designs)

Study	Place	N Mixed/All White	Grade Level	How Desegregated?	Design	Comparison	Controls	Pretest/Posttest[a]	IQ or Verbal	Reading	Math	General or Unspecified	Remarks
Banks and DiPasquale (1969)	Buffalo, N.Y.	c. 1000	5-7	Receive bused black pupils	Four-celled	1-year gain versus gain of previous children	No	MAT/MAT			0		No significance tests reported. Desegregation has no negative effect on performance on MAT paragraph meaning
Boland (1968)	Five major Connecticut cities	All pupils in 47 elementary schools; 1/3 seniors in 13 H.S.	6, 12	Neighborhood	Cross-sectional	School % black	Father's education and occupation	None/HN	–				No significance tests reported. Henmon-Nelson IQ tends to be lower in majority-black schools in grade 6, not in grade 12
Bryant (1968)	Angleton, Tex.	751	8-11	Segregated school closed	Longitudinal	1-year gain post-desegregation	Sex	STAP/STAP				– 0	Significant loss relative to norms on STAP. No significant difference in GPA
Dambacher (1971)	Berkeley, Cal.	3000 + (all whites in system)	1-6	Total system: K-3, white receive; 4-6, white bused	Longitudinal	2-year gain: post- versus pre-desegregation	No	SAT/SAT CAT/CAT					No significance tests reported. Whites continue to show high gains on SAT and adjusted CAT reading tests

Chart A-4. Studies of white achievement (all designs) (Contd.)

Study	Place	N Mixed/All White	Grade Level	How Desegregated?	Design	Comparison	Controls	Pretest/ Posttest[a]	IQ or Verbal	Reading	Math	General or Unspecified	Remarks
Graves and Bedell (1967)	White Plains, N.Y.	129/150	3-6	Receive transferred blacks	Longitudinal	3-year gain: post- versus predesegregation	No	SAT/SAT	+ 0 −	+ 0			Progress of integrated equal to or better than that of formerly segregated in all areas except word meaning, which was slightly lower
Heller et al. (1972)	Westport, Conn.	169/58	1-3	Receive bused black pupils from central city	Four-celled	1-year gain: desegregated versus segregated	No	MAT/MAT				0	No significance tests. No adverse effects on the white receiving pupils
Hsia (1971)	Evanston, Ill.	¼ whites in city	1,2,4,5	Receive transferred blacks	Longitudinal	3-year gain versus national norms	No	CPT/CPT STEP/STEP				0 +	No significant difference except greater gain for those reverse-bused to laboratory school
Jonsson (1967); Sullivan (1968)	Berkeley, Cal.	4000+	1-6	Receive bused black pupils	Four-celled	1-year gain: post- versus pre-desegregation	No	SAT/SAT					No significance tests reported. Whites continue to show large gains
Laurent (1969)	Tacoma, Wash.	40/40	1-8	Neighborhood	Four-celled	3-year gain: majority black versus majority white	IQ, SES, Age	STEP/STEP				0 +	No school effect, though whites in majority white school scored higher on 1 out of 12 comparisons — the Primary Composite

Outcomes for Desegregated

Study	Location	N	Grades	Assignment	Design	Comparison	Controls (IQ/SES)	Test (pre/post)	Result		Comments
Long (1968)	Northern suburb	43/50	K-2	Neighborhood	Cross-sectional	Mixed versus all-white	No	None/ITBS	0		No significant difference between pupils in mixed and all-white schools
Mahan (1968)	Hartford, Conn.	2 samples drawn from 6 schools	K-5	Receive bused black pupils	Four-celled	1-year gain: post- versus pre-desegregation	No	ITBS/ITBS	+		A trend for white pupils in class with transferred blacks to do somewhat better (not significant) than segregated whites.
Mayer et al. (1973)	Goldsboro, N. Carolina	111	3-5	Total system reassignment	Longitudinal	Gain versus national norms	None	SAT/SAT		+	Significant gain from grade 3 to 5 relative to national norms (gain = 3.1 on math and verbal standardized scores)
Mayer et al. (1973)	Goldsboro, N. Carolina	47/29/33	3-5	Total system reassignment	Four-celled	2-year gain: much versus some versus little desegregation experience	Teacher open/traditional; neighborhood SES	SAT/SAT		+ −	Significant gain in verbal and math for all, but greater gains for those with little desegregation experience than for those with much
Maynor (1970)	Hoke County N. Carolina	608	6-12	Receive transferred blacks	Longitudinal	1-year gain: post- versus predesegregation	Teacher's race, IQ	CAT/CAT	0		Whites and Indians performed equally well preintegrated and postintegration on CAT language test
McCullough (1972)	Goldsboro, N. Carolina	Entire class (c.4000)	7,8,9,11 cohort	Total system desegregation	Longitudinal	2 year gain post-desegregation	No	SAT/SAT	0	0	No significant gain or loss in SAT reading test following desegregation
Moorefield (1967)	Kansas City, Mo.	720	4,6	Receive transferred	Longitudinal	1-year gain: pre- versus post-	No (desegregated of	ITBS/ITBS		−	Decline in reading achievement gain; not attributed to the presence of

Chart A-4. Studies of white achievement (all designs) (Contd.)

Study	Place	N Mixed/All White	Grade Level	How Desegregated?	Design	Comparison	Controls	Pretest/ Posttest[a]	IQ or Verbal	Read- ing	Math	General or Unspecified	Remarks
				black pupils		desegregation	higher SES)						bused blacks since there was a general decline throughout the school system
Prichard (1969)	Chapel Hill, N. Carolina	420/210	5,7,9	Total system desegregation	Four-celled	1- and 2-year gain post- versus pre-desegregation	No	STEP/STEP		0	+, 0		Significant gain in math, grade 5; no significant difference in other years or other subjects
Purl and Dawson (1973)	Riverside, Cal.	All in system (c. 1200)	K-3	Receive bused pupils	Longitu- dinal	Mean achievement relative to national norms, 1965-1972	No	MRT/MRT SAT/SAT CPT/CPT	+	0			Achievement of K-1 rose steadily and significantly, 1966-1970. Achievement of grade 2 rose slightly. Achievement of grade 3 decreased
St. John and Lewis (1971)	Boston, Mass.	497	6	Neighborhood, open enroll- ment, and some busing	Four-celled	School % white, grades 1-6	Sex, SES, school SES, Grades 1-6	MAT/MAT	−	−	−	0	Significant negative relation with school % black on arithmetic, read- ing, and IQ, not GPA

Study	Location	N	Grades	Program	Design	Comparison	Controls	Tests	Effect	Results
School Board (1970)	Rochester, N.Y.	92/97	3-6	Voluntary busing to inner city	Four-celled	Whites in experimental school (20% white) versus whites in neighborhood schools (72-93% white)	No	NYAT/NYAT ITBS/ITBS	0	No significant difference in achievement trends for the two groups of white students
School Board (1972)	Shaker Heights, O.	29 citywide norms	4-6	Voluntary transfer to formerly all black school	Four-celled	7 month gain: transfer versus average of all pupils	No	SAT/SAT	+ / −	Whites reassigned to predominantly black school gained more in grades 4 and 6, not grade 5. No significance tests
Scudder and Jurs (1971)	Denver, Col.	909/802	24	Receive transferred black pupils	Four-celled	1-year gain: desegregated versus segregated	IQ, SES, Sex	SAT/SAT	0 / −	Significant loss in math in grades 2 and 4; no significant difference in 11 out of 13 other tests
Slone (1968)	New York City	34/57	4	Paired schools	Four-celled	1-year gain: transfer versus nontransfer	Matched on IQ, read-achievement, ethnicity	MAT/MAT ITBS/ITBS	0 / 0	No significant difference on any achievement test between transferred and nontransferred
Stallings (1959)	Louisville, Ky.	All whites in city: 7771/8862	2,6,8	Dual system eliminated	Longitudinal	2 year gain: post versus predesegregation	No	CAT/CAT SAT/SAT	0	Significant gains for whites whether in school with a very few blacks or a substantial percentage of blacks

Chart A-4. Studies of white achievement (all designs) (Concl.)

Study	Place	N Integrated/Segregated	Grade Levels	How Desegregated?	Design	Comparison	Controls	Pretest/Posttest[a]	IQ or Verbal	Reading	Math	General or Unspecified	Remarks
Zdep and Joyce (1969)	Newark and Verona, N.J.	12/7 classes	1-2	Received bused pupils	Four-celled	1-year gain versus all-white classes	No	MRT/CPT CPT/CPT				0	No significant difference in achievement gains between classes that did and did not receive bused blacks

[a]
CAT: California Achievement Test
CSS: California Survey Series
CPT: Cooperative Primary Tests
DAT: Differential Aptitude Test
GRT: Gates Reading Test
HN: Henmon-Nelson IQ Test
ITBS: Iowa Test of Basic Skills
KA: Kuhlman-Anderson
LCRT: Lee-Clark Reading Readiness Test
LIPS: Leiter International Performance Scale

LT: Lorge-Thorndike Intelligence Tests
MAT: Metropolitan Achievement Test
MRT: Metropolitan Readiness Test
NYAT: New York State Achievement Tests
RPT: Reading Prognosis Test
STAP: Scannel Test of Academic Progress
STEP: Sequential Tests of Educational Progress
SAT: Stanford Achievement Test
WISC: Wechsler Intelligence Scale for Children
PAT: Progressive Achievement Test

Chart A-5. Desegregation and minority group anxiety

Study	Sample (N; Grade; Place)	Definition	Instrument	Design	Comparison	Controls	Outcome Effect	Outcome Significant	Remarks
Bienvenu (1968)	40/40 males; grades 9-11; Florida	General anxiety	Taylor Manifest Anxiety Scale	Four-celled	1-year change: transfer versus nontransfer	Age, IQ, grade, residence, parental education and occupation	0	No	Significant increase in anxiety for both experimental and control groups; no significant difference in anxiety between the two groups
Carrigan (1969)	63; grades 2-5; Ann Arbor, Mich.	General and school anxiety	Sarason Scale; questionnaire; school attitudes card sort	Longitudinal	1-year change: pre- versus posttransfer	Sex	− +	No No	Transfer group showed a slight increase (not significant) in school-related anxiety and a decrease (not significant) in general anxiety
Lammers (1969)	15/15 Indians; J.H.S.; central New York state	Test anxiety	Sarason Scale	Cross-sectional	Desegregated versus segregated elementary education	IQ	0	No	No significant difference between groups on test anxiety
Mahan (1963)	197/244; grades K-5; "Project Concern" Hartford, Conn.	General and test anxiety	Sarason Scales	Cross-sectional (change score not reported)	Bused to suburbs versus nontransfer	Random classes transferred (no other controls)	0	No	No significant difference between groups on either test

Chart A-5. Desegregation and minority group anxiety (Concl.)

Study	Sample (N; Grade; Place)	Definition	Instrument	Design	Comparison	Controls	Effect	Significant	Remarks
Meketon (1966)	89; grades 5–6, 2 communities in Kentucky	General anxiety	3 performance tests sensitive to anxiety	Cross-sectional (comparison after 8 months of desegregation)	School A: Segregated; School B: Integrated peacefully; School C: Integrated after controversy	Schools A and B matched on IQ, scholastic records, grade, age, and SES; C pupils not matched and have higher IQ	+ 0	No No	School C scored somewhat higher (not significant) than A and B on performance tests. No significant difference between A and B
Slone (1968)	32/80; grade 4; New York City	General and test anxiety	Sarason Scales	Cross-sectional (change score not reported)	1-year change: Desegregated versus segregated	Matched on IQ, reading, and SES	– 0	No No	Desegregated showed (almost significant) higher general anxiety than segregated and no difference on test anxiety
Wessman (1969)	23/23 males (38 black, 6 Puerto Rican, 2 white); high school; ABC Program, national	General anxiety	Cattell HSPQ	Four-celled	2-year change: Desegregated versus controls	IQ, race, age	–	Yes	ABC students showed a significant increase in overall anxiety with no significant changes for the matched non-ABC controls

Chart A-6. Desegregation and minority group self-concept, self-esteem, and sense of control

Study	Sample (N; Grade; Place)	Definition	Instrument	Design		Controls	Outcome		Remarks
				Design	Comparison		Effect	Significant	
Aberdeen (1969)	40 blacks; grades K-3; Ann Arbor, Mich.	Self-esteem	Coopersmith	Longitudinal	Predesegregation versus 1-year postdesegregation versus 3-year postdesegregation	No	0	No	Self-esteem rose during first year of desegregation and then fell to a point near predesegregation level but the changes were not significant
Anderson (1966)	150; grades 4-6; Nashville, Tenn.	Personal adjustment	California Test of Personality	Cross-sectional	Desegregated versus segregated	Age, IQ, intact family (not SES)	0	No	No significant difference in level or pattern of adjustment
Armor (1972a)	130/38 (METCO); grades 7-12; Boston, Mass.	Academic self-concept	Questionnaire	Four-celled	2-year change: METCO (bused to suburbs) versus non-METCO siblings	Family background	— —	Yes No	METCO pupils had significantly lower self-concept than siblings. Self-concept declined for METCO pupils, but not significantly
Bachman (1970)	73/72/111 males; grade 10; national	Self-esteem; academic self-concept; sense of control	Interview questionnaire	Cross-sectional	73 north integrated, 72 north segregated, 111 south segregated	SES, IQ	—	No	Self-esteem is higher for both segregated groups than integrated northerners; academic self-concept tends to be highest for segregated southerners, lowest for integrated northerners; no difference on sense of control

Chart A-6. Desegregation and minority group self-concept, self-esteem, and sense of control (Contd.)

Study	Sample (N; Grade; Place)	Definition	Design				Outcome		
			Instrument	Design	Comparison	Controls	Effect	Significant	Remarks
Barber (1968)	50/50; grade 8; Rochester, N.Y.	Racial group self-esteem	Davidoff's Prejudice Questionnaire	Cross-sectional	Open enrollment versus segregated school	Alike in SES and residence	—	No	Slightly higher self-esteem for the segregated. The lower self-concept of the desegregated attributed to community hostility
Bienvenu (1968)	40/40 males; grades 9-11; Florida	General self-concept	Bill Index of Adjustment and Values	Four-celled	1-year change: transfer versus nontransfer	Age, IQ, grade, residence, parental education and occupation	— 0	Yes No	Control group had significantly higher self-concept. No significant change in self-concept for either group over the year
Carrigan (1969)	93; elementary; Ann Arbor, Mich.	Self-esteem	Grades 1-2: Picture sort; Grades 3-6: Coopersmith	Longitudinal	1-year change: pretransfer versus post-transfer	Sex	0	No	Self-esteem unaffected by transfer
Coleman (1966)	EEOS data; grades 9-12; national	Academic self-concept; sense of control	Questionnaire	Cross-sectional	School % white	No	— +	Yes Yes	The higher the school % white, the lower is academic self-concept and the higher is sense of control
Denmark (1970	87; elementary; Manhasset, N.Y.	General self-concept	Semi-projective, close-ended test,	Longitudinal	1-year change: pretransfer	Sex	+ +	Yes No	Male self-concept in grades 1 and 2 improved significant-

Study	Sample	Variable measured	Instrument	Design	Comparison	Controls		Significant difference	Results
			individually administered		versus post-transfer				...ly; females improved but not significantly
Evans (1969)	99/99; grades 4-6; Texas	Personal and social adjustment	California Test of Personality	Four-celled	1-year change: desegregated versus segregated	IQ, sex, grade, classroom % black, SES	—	Yes	Integrated showed substantial loss, mostly in social adjustment; Segregated also showed some loss in social adjustment, but a significant overall gain
Gardner et al. (1970)	Target sample: 130/130; grades 6-8; Chicago parochial	Academic self-concept	Semantic Differential	Cross-sectional	Voluntary bused (for 2 years) versus non-bused	No	—	—[a]	Bused blacks rate themselves lower on certain factors than do nonbused blacks
Garth (1969)	44/50; high school; Louisville, Ky.	Self-perception	Semantic Differential	Cross-sectional	Voluntary transfer versus non-transfer	SES (IQ and achievement of integrated higher)	—	Yes	Transferees define white people and integrated H.S. as more similar to "Me" and rate them more favorably, but "Me" less favorably
Gerard and Miller (1971)	225; elementary; Riverside, Cal.	Personality traits	Series of instruments	Longitudinal	3-year change: postdesegregation	Sex	0	No	No significant change revealed by analyses to date
Griffin (1969)	32/32; grades 4-6; Tulsa, Okla.	General self-concept	SRA Digest Attitude Inventory	Cross-sectional	1-year change: desegregated versus segregated	Matched on SES, IQ, and sex	0	No	No significant difference on items involving attitude to self

167

Chart A-6. Desegregation and minority group self-concept, self-esteem, and a sense of control (Contd.)

Study	Sample (N; Grade; Place)	Design					Outcome		
		Definition	Instrument	Design	Comparison	Controls	Effect	Significant	Remarks
Harootunian (1968)	46/138; grade 9; rural Delaware	Self-esteem	Self-social symbol tasks	Cross-sectional	Open Enrollment versus segregated	Age, sex	−	Yes	Desegregated, especially boys, have lower self-esteem
Hsia (1971)	All blacks in city; grades 3-5; Evanston, Ill.	Academic self-concept	Questionnaire (Campbell's)	Longitudinal	3-year gain	No	−	—[a]	Some decrease in self-concept of transferred black students after desegregation
Jessup (1967)	20/203; grades 2 and 5; New York City	Self-image	Drawings	Cross-sectional	Integrated versus segregated	SES	+	Yes	Integrated showed significantly higher self-concept than segregated; integrated in grade 5 have higher self-concept than those in grade 2; no difference between grades for segregated
Knight (1970)	179/162; seniors; North Carolina	Satisfaction with self	Gordon's Survey of Interpersonal Values	Cross-sectional	Pupils in 4 integrated versus 4 segregated high schools	Sex, SES (all have low SES)	0	No	No significant difference on interpersonal values; no significant difference on satisfaction with self

Author (year)	Sample	Self-concept variable	Instrument	Design	Comparison	Controls	Sign	Significant	Results
Lammers (1969)	15/15 Indians: J.H.S.; Central New York State	Self-concept of ability	Self-social symbol task	Cross-sectional	Desegregated versus segregated elementary education	IQ	0	No	No significant difference on self-concept
Lockwood (1966)	217; grade 6; upstate New York	Self-esteem	Questionnaire	Cross-sectional	Integrated versus segregated	No	0 / +	No / Yes	No significant difference except on item, "I am pretty happy." The integrated were happier
McPartland (1968)	Over 4000 from EEOS data, grade 9; Metropolitan northeast	Self-image; sense of control	Questionnaire: "If I could change I would be someone different" — Disagree	Cross-sectional	Class % white; earliest grade with whites	SES, achievement	+ / 0	Yes / No	Both class % white and earliest grade with whites contribute to sense of control, but neither contribute to self-image
McWhirt (1967)	38/38; grade 10; South	Evaluative rating of self	Semantic Differential	Four-celled	8 month change: newly desegregated versus segregated	Matched on sex, age, IQ, SES, aspirations, and family size	+ / –	No / No	Self-concept of desegregated females rose relative to segregated females; that of desegregated males rose, but not as much as that of segregated males
Meketon (1966)	89; grades 5-6; two communities in Kentucky	Self-esteem	Coopersmith	Cross-sectional (comparison after 8 months of desegregation)	School A: Segregated; School B: Integrated peacefully; School C: Integrated after controversy	Schools A and B matched on IQ, scholastic records, grade, age, and SES; C pupils not matched and had higher IQ	–	No	Higher self-esteem in schools A and C than in B

169

Chart A-6. Desegregation and minority group self-concept, self-esteem, and sense of control (Contd.)

Study	Sample (N; Grade; Place)	Design					Outcome		
		Definition	Instrument	Design	Comparison	Controls	Effect	Significant	Remarks
Moorefield (1967)	104/321; grades 4 and 6; Kansas City, Mo.	Academic self-esteem	Questionnaire	Cross-sectional	Desegregated (bused for 1 year) versus segregated	No (desegregated school of higher SES)	0	—[a]	No significance tests were made and no clear trends were apparent
Perry (1973)	125/103; 1970 seniors; ABC Program; national	Self-esteem; sense of control	Questionnaire	Four-celled	Sophomore-senior difference; ABC versus matched non-ABC pupils	Community size, father presence, parental education and income, public school GPA, GSAT score	+ 0	Yes No	Self-esteem rose from grade 10 to 12 for ABC but not for non-ABC pupils; sense of control rose from grade 10 to 12 for both ABC and non-ABC pupils
Powell and Fuller (1970)	149/155; J.H.S.; central southern city	General self-concept	Tennessee Self-Concept Scale	Cross-sectional	Desegregated versus segregated	No	—	—[a]	Higher self-concept for segregated; desegregated boys scored higher than desegregated girls; results attributed to black community leadership
Rosenberg and Simmons	114/336; grades 7-12; Baltimore, Md.	Self-esteem	Interviews; 6-item Guttman Scale	Cross-sectional	Pupils in predominantly white versus pre-	Family structure	— —	No Yes	In junior high self-esteem tends to be lower and in senior high self-esteem is signifi-

Study	Sample	Measure	Instrument	Design	Independent variable	Controls	Effect	Significant	Findings
(1971)					dominantly black schools				cantly lower in predominantly white schools, but only for children from separated or never-married families
St. John (1969)	1380; grade 9; Pittsburgh, Pa.	Self-esteem sense of control	Semantic Differential; Coleman Items; Rosenberg Scale	Cross-sectional	School % white (9); school % white (1-9)	SES, sex, high school	0	No	Nonsignificant curvilinear trend toward highest scores for 40-60 school % white
St. John (1971)	416; grade 6; Boston, Mass.	Academic self-concept; general self-concept; sense of control	Ladder Semantic Differential; Coleman Items	Cross-sectional	Class % white (6); school % white (1-5)	Sex, IQ, SES	— + 0	Yes Yes No	Present class % white has negative effect on self-concept (academic and general). Past school % white has positive effect on both. Neither affects sense of control
Scott (1969)	30/30; grade 7; Oklahoma City	Self-esteem	Coopersmith	Cross-sectional	Integrated versus segregated after 2 years	No	0	No	No significant difference but desegregated tend to be less dissatisfied with current personal status
Slone (1968)	32/80; grade 4; New York City	Attitudes	Morse Questionnaire	Cross-sectional	Desegregated versus segregated	Matched on IQ, reading, SES	0	No	No significant difference between groups on any attitudes

Chart A-6. Desegregation and minority group self-concept, self-esteem, and sense of control (Contd.)

Study	Sample (N; Grade; Place)	Definition	Instrument	Design	Comparison	Controls	Effect	Significant	Remarks
				Design			**Outcome**		
Strauss (1967)	100 black and Puerto Rican; grades 2-3; New York City	School self-concept	Questionnaire	Four-celled	½- to 1½-year change: paired versus predominantly black school	Similar age and academic achievement within grade level	+	Yes	Paired pupils had significantly higher self-concept than segregated; no significant difference between those desegregated for 1½ years (Grade 3) and ½ year (Grade 2
Taylor (1967)	15/21/22; grades 6-7; Maryland and Delaware	Self-esteem	Self-social symbol tasks	Four-celled	Change: early desegregated versus 1-year desegregated versus segregated	No	−	No	Desegregated tend to decrease in self-esteem after initial rise; significant decrease in size of group identified with and increase in identifying with friends
U.S. Commission on Civil Rights (1967a)	EEOS data; grade 9; metropolitan northeast	Sense of control	Questionnaire	Cross-sectional	Class % white	Individual and school SES	+	Yes	The higher the classroom % white, with individual and school SES controlled, the greater is the sense of control
Walker (1968)	46/46; grades 7-8; Dade County,	Self-concept as a learner;	Maryland Scale; Tennessee Scale	Four-celled	2-year change: desegregated	SES (measured through home interviews)	+ 0	Yes No	Middle class general self concept decreases less in

Author	Sample	Measure	Design	Comparison	Controls			Results
	Fla.	general self-concept		versus segregated				integrated school in first year than in segregated schools; lower class overall self-concept increases in second year in integrated school
Wellman (1970; 1971)	1380; grade 9; Pittsburgh, Pa.	Self-identity as a student or as Black; "Who Am I?" test	Cross-sectional	School % black	SES	0		Significantly higher self-identification as student in blackest and whitest schools at all except highest SES levels; less self-identification as black in all-black schools
Wessman (1969)	75 males; high school; ABC Program, national	Self-acceptance: Gough CPI sense of well-being	Longitudinal	2 year change: desegregated	No	+ / +	Yes / No	ABC students showed a significant increase on self-acceptance and a slight increase (not significant) on sense of well-being
D.E. Williams (1968)	81/100; preschool; New York City and suburb	Self-concept; "self-worth along combined dimensions"	Cross-sectional	Inner city segregated versus long-integrated suburban community	Only father's presence (integrated have higher SES and integrated girls have higher IQ)	+ / 0	Yes / No	Significant positive difference for integrated girls, not boys

Chart A-6. Desegregation and minority group self-concept, self-esteem, and sense of control (Concl.)

| Study | Sample (N; Grade; Place) | Design | | | | | Outcome | | |
		Definition	Instrument	Design	Comparison	Controls	Effect	Significant	Remarks
Williams and Byars (1970)	22/31/41; grade 11; deep South	Physical, moral, personal, family, and social self	Tennessee Self-Concept Scale	Four-celled	1-year change: School A; newly de-segregated versus B: segregated pupils and integrated faculty versus C: segregated pupils and faculty	No	+ 0	Yes No	Significant gain for integrated only on physical self; over-all gain greatest in segre-gated school with inte-grated faculty
Zirkel and Moses (1971)	40 black, 40 Puerto Rican, 40 white; grades 5-6; Connecticut	Self; social self; school self	Coopersmith	Cross-sectional	Three schools with different % white, black and Puerto Rican	Sex, SES, IQ	— —	No Yes	Each ethnic group tends to have lower self-concept in school in which it is the minority; the differ-ence is significant for Puerto Ricans

[a] No significance tests reported.

Chart A-7. Desegregation and minority group aspiration

Study	Sample (N; Grade; Place)	Definition	Instrument	Design	Comparison	Controls	Outcome Effect	Outcome Significant	Remarks
Armor (1967)	EEOS data; grades 9-12; metropolitan areas, national	% planning college	Questionnaire	Cross-sectional	Integrated versus segregated schools	Sex, SES, IQ, school SES, region	+ −	—[a]	Strongest positive effect for low SES, upper ability grade 9 males in northeast; for all other groups, the segregated had highest aspiration
Armor (1972a)	132/34 METCO; grades 7-12; Boston, Mass.	Educational and occupational aspiration	Questionnaire	Four-celled	2-year change: METCO (bused to suburbs) versus non-METCO siblings	Family background	− −	Yes No	Educational aspirations of bused pupils declined significantly relative to siblings; occupational aspirations of bused pupils declined but not significantly relative to siblings
Bachman (1970)	73/73/11 males; grade 10; national	Educational and occupational aspiration	Interview questionnaire	Cross-sectional	Southern segregated versus northern segregated versus northern integrated	SES, IQ	−	Yes	Aspirations are lowest for integrated northerners and highest for segregated southerners, with segregated northerners between the two

175

Chart A-7. Desegregation and minority group aspiration (Contd.)

Study	Sample (N; Grade; Place)	Definition	Instrument	Design	Comparison	Controls	Effect	Significant	Remarks
Blake (1960)	59/59; high school; suburb of large midwestern city	Aspiration	Difference between actual and predicted class rank in English	Cross-sectional	Integrated versus segregated schools	IQ, SES, achievement	−	No	Aspirations of segregated blacks were higher than integrated blacks, but the difference was not significant
Boland (1968)	All grade 6 pupils in 47 schools; 1/3 seniors in 13 high schools (grade 12); five major cities in Connecticut	Educational and occupational aspiration	Questionnaire	Cross-sectional	School % black	Father's education and occupation	− +	—[a]	No significance test; as school % black rises, educational aspiration tends to decline and occupational aspiration tends to rise
Bryant (1968)	102; grades 8-11; Angleton, Tex.	Dropout rate	School records	Longitudinal	Difference in annual dropout rate after desegregation	Sex	−	Yes	Highly significant increase in dropout rates, especially among males, in the year following desegregation
Chesler and Segal (1967)	197/75; grades 9-12; Alabama	Occupational aspiration	Interview after first year desegregation	Cross-sectional	Desegregated versus segregated	No	0 +	—[a]	No significance tests. No difference in aspirations; desegregated have higher expectations

Study	Sample	Variable	Instrument	Design	Comparison	Controls	Sign	Significant	Results
Curtis (1968)	164/219; grades 9-12; Dade County, Fla.	Vocational aspiration	Vocational interest checklist	Cross-sectional	Desegregated versus segregated	SES, GPA, achievement	+	Yes	Desegregated chose professional, technical, and managerial jobs significantly more often
Danahy (1971)	41/41; grades 2-6; Minneapolis, Minn.	Absenteeism	School records	Longitudinal	Pre- versus posttransfer	Grade level	0	No	No significant difference between pre- and posttransfer absence of transfer pupils
Falk, Cosby, and Wright (1973)	All pupils grade 10 in 22 H.S.; 3 rural counties in Texas	Educational aspiration and expectation	Questionnaire	Four-celled	Desegregated versus segregated 2-6 years after desegregation	All of low SES	0	No	No significant difference (short run or long run) in educational aspiration or expectation of segregated and desegregated; desegregated perceive race and schools attended as significantly more detrimental
Fisher (1970)	Boys of 4 schools; high school; Oklahoma City	Educational plan	Questionnaire (Wilson's)	Cross-sectional	1-year change after desegregation	No	0	No	No significant difference in educational plans of blacks in predominantly black, 36% black, or predominantly white schools
Heller (1964)	67/98 Mexican-American boys; grade 12; Los Angeles, Cal.	Occupational aspirations	Questionnaire	Cross-sectional	Mexican-American in minority versus in majority	No	+ –	Yes	Mexican-Americans in majority-white schools aspire significantly more to nonmanual occupations and significantly less to be self-employed

Chart A-7. Desegregation and minority group aspiration (Contd.)

Study	Sample (N; Grade; Place)	Design — Definition	Design — Instrument	Design — Design	Design — Comparison	Design — Controls	Outcome — Effect	Outcome — Significant	Outcome — Remarks
Knight (1970)	179/162 seniors; North Carolina	Occupational choice; Educational plans	Questionnaire	Cross-sectional	Integrated versus segregated	SES, Sex, (all of low SES)	+ − 0	No Yes No	Integrated males (not significantly) and segregated females (significantly) have higher educational plans than segregated males and integrated females. No significant difference on occupational aspirations
Lewis (1970)	1262 males; grade 12 in 84 H.S.; North Carolina	Occupational expectation	Questionnaire	Cross-sectional	"Socially integrated" versus "physically integrated" versus segregated	SES, school size, rural or urban community	+ −	Yes No	Occupational expectation is negatively related to physical integration but significant only for classes 18-63% nonwhite, and positively (significantly) related to social integration
Lindsay and Gottlieb (1969)	Males in 55 H.S.; grade 12; national (NORC)	Educational and occupational aspirations and expectations	Questionnaire	Cross-sectional	High school % black		+		The higher is the school % white, the higher is the aspiration and expectation

Study	Sample	Dependent variable	Instrument	Design	Comparison	Controls			Results
McWhirt (1967)	38/38; grade 10; South	Academic aspiration	Semantic differential rating of a good education	Four-celled	8-month change: newly desegregated versus segregated	Matched on Sex, age, IQ, SES, family size, and aspiration	+	Yes	A significantly greater increase in the rating of "a good education" in the integrated than in the segregated schools
Perry (1973)	47/47 blacks; 1967 H.S. graduates; ABC program, national	College entrance; college selection	Questionnaire	Cross-sectional	2- to 4-year desegregated ABC versus matched non-ABC	Community size, father presence, parental education and income, public school GPA, GSAT score	+ +	Yes Yes	94% of ABC and 62% of non-ABC entered college; ABC attended more selective colleges than did controls
Perry (1973)	125/103; 1970 seniors; ABC program, national	Educational and occupaginal aspiration	Questionnaire	Four-celled	Sophomore-senior difference: ABC versus matched non-ABC pupils	Community size, father presence, parental education and income, public school GPA, Gsat score	0	No	Aspiration rose from grade 10 to 12 for both ABC and non-ABC pupils
Prichard (1969)	90/90/90; grades 5, 7, and 9; Chapel Hill, N.C.	Absenteeism	School records	Longitudinal	Change: predesegregated versus 1-year post-desegregated versus 2-year postdesegregated	No	–	No	For black boys (grade 7 and 9) absenteeism increased in the second year of desegregation, but not significantly
St. John (1966)	230; grade 11; New Haven, Conn.	Educational plans; occupational preference	Questionnaire	Cross-sectional	School % white (grades 1-9)	Birthplace, SES	–	No	No significant relation but a trend toward higher aspirations for segregated

179

Chart A-7. Desegregation and minority group aspiration (Concl.)

Study	Sample (N; Grade; Place)	Design					Outcome		
		Definition	Instrument	Design	Comparison	Controls	Effect	Significant	Remarks
St. John (1973)	1388; grade 9; Pittsburgh, Pa.	Educational aspiration and expectation; occupational aspiration	Questionnaire	Cross-sectional	School % white (grades 1-9)	Sex, SES, IQ	— — 0	Yes Yes No	Especially for high-IQ males, segregated have significantly higher educational aspirations and expectations; no difference on occupational aspiration
St. John (1971)	412; grade 6; Boston, Mass.	Educational aspiration	Questionnaire	Cross-sectional	Class % white (6); school % white (1-5)	No	+ —	No No	Slight positive relation between classroom % white (6) and educational aspiration; slight negative relation between school % white (1-5) and educational aspiration
TenHouten et al. (1971)	624 Mexican-Americans grade 12 in 5 H.S.; Los Angeles, Cal.	College plans	Questionnaire	Cross-sectional	School % Mexican-American (in 5 H.S. 11-65% Mexican-American	SES, IQ, parental and peer aspiration	—	No	More likely to develop college plans in schools dominated by own groups, but effect slight when other variables are controlled
Veroff and Peele	165/409; grades K-5; Ann	Autonomous and social	Graded series of tasks	Four-celled	1-year change: transfer	Age, sex	—	Yes	Transferred boys increased significantly more in auton-

| (1969) | Arbor, Mich. | comparison, achievement motivation | | versus non-transfer | | | omous achievement motivation than nontransferred boys; no significant difference for girls; desegregated older boys show less over-aspiration as measured by social comparison test |
| Wilson (1961) | 20/81 males; grade 6; Berkeley, Cal. | Educational and occupational aspiration | Cross-sectional | Schools in Foothills (14% black) versus schools in Flats (66% black) | No | —[a] | Aspiration higher in the Flats |

[a] No significance tests reported.

Chart A-8. School desegregation and interracial attitudes of white and black pupils

Study	Sample (N; Grade; Place)	Design					Outcome				Remarks
		Instrument	Design	Comparison	Type and Years of Desegregation	Controls	Whites		Blacks		
							Direction	Significant	Direction	Significant	
Armor (1972a)	135/36 black; grades 11-12; METCO, Boston, Mass.	Questionnaire on attitudes	Four-celled	Bused versus nonbused siblings	7 months; voluntary for blacks	Family background			−	Yes	Significant increase in separatist ideology and decrease in interaction with whites
Barber (1968)	50/50 white, 50/50 black; grade 8 in 3 schools; Rochester, N.Y.	Davidoff's Prejudice Questionnaires; interview on attitudes	Cross-sectional	A: Open Enrollment; B: segregated black; C: segregated white	1 year; voluntary for blacks	Alike in SES and residence	−	Yes	−	Yes	Both whites and blacks less hostile in the segregated schools than in school A where the community is hostile to open enrollment
Campbell (1956)	746 white; grades 8, 10, 12; Oak Ridge, Tenn.	Questionnaire; Guttman Scales on attitudes	Longitudinal	Change after 1 year of desegregation	5 months; 9½ months between tests	No	− +	Yes			Significant negative change greater for desegregated than segregated, especially for those in classes with blacks; positive change is greater when both parents and friends are prodesegregation and also when whites claim blacks as friends

Study	Sample	Measure/Instrument	Design	Comparison	Duration/Basis	Controls					Findings
Carrigan (1969)	31/212 white and 132/195 black; grades K-5; Ann Arbor, Mich.	Questionnaire; social distance scale; school attitudes card sort; interviews	Longitudinal	Change: transfer versus nontransfer	1 year; systemwide	No (race of classmates not controlled)	−	Yes	−	Yes	Significant decline in acceptance by classmates for both whites and blacks in nontransfer group, and for only blacks in transfer group
Crooks (1970)	17/17 white, 17/17 black; preschool: age 4-5; New Brunswick, Can.	Choice of brown or white doll	Cross-sectional	Integrated preschool versus no preschool	1 year; voluntary	No (both live in integrated neighborhood)	+	Yes	−	Yes	Both whites and blacks show greater preference for black doll if they had attended integrated preschool
Dentler and Elkins (1967)	1806 white/424 black (approx); grades 3-6; northern metropolitan area	Bogardus Social Distance Scale; Racial Opinions Index	Cross-sectional	School % white	1 year; neighborhood	(Races not analyzed separately)	−	Yes			Prejudice increases as % black of school increases
Evans (1969)	99/99 blacks; grades 4-6; Texas	Purdue Racial Attitude Scale	Four-celled	1-year change: desegregated versus segregated	1 year; systemwide	IQ, grade, sex, class % black		Yes	−	Yes	Segregated gained significantly in cross-racial acceptance, integrated decreased slightly
Gardner et al. (1970)	Target sample: 130/130 white and black; grades 6-8; Chicago parochial school	Semantic differential on attitudes	Four-celled	Volunteer bused black versus nonbused black; integrated white versus segregated white	2 years +; voluntary for blacks	No	+	Yes	+	Yes	Both whites and blacks have better image of each other in integrated situation

Chart A-8. School desegregation and interracial attitudes of white and black pupils (Contd.)

Study	Sample (N; Grade; Place)	Design					Outcome				Remarks
		Instrument	Design	Comparison	Type and Years of Desegregation	Controls	Whites		Blacks		
							Direction	Signif-icant	Direction	Signif-icant	
Garth (1969)	44/50 black; high school; Louisville, Ky.	Semantic differential	Cross-sectional	Transfer versus nontransfer	1 year; voluntary for blacks	SES (transferees have higher IQ)			+	Yes	Transferees define white people and integrated high school more favorably
Herman (1967, 1970)	66/150 black, 27/107 white; grade 6; New Haven, Conn.	Social distance	Cross-sectional	Integrated versus segregated neighborhood school	Neighborhood	No	−	Yes	0		Desegregated whites significantly less tolerant than segregated whites; no significant difference for blacks
Kurokawa (1971)	100 white, 100 black, 100 Japanese-American; grades 4-5; Sacramento, Cal.	Open-ended description of other race	Cross-sectional	White-dominated school versus mixed school	Neighborhood	No	+	Yes	−	Yes	In white-dominated school, significantly more whites, blacks, and Japanese-Americans gave other group negative traits than in mixed schools
Lombardi (1962)	265/79 white; grades 10-11;	Attitude scale	Four-celled	Pre- and post-desegregation	7 months; system-	Sex, SES, IQ, religion	0				No significant change in experimental or control group;

Study	Sample	Measure	Design	Comparison	Duration	Controls	Direction	Significant	Results
	small city in Maryland			versus control	wide				positive change related to mother's education, negative change related to decline in GPA; change and degree of classroom contact unrelated
McPartland (1968)	Over 4000 white and black; from EEOS data, grade 9; Metropolitan Northeast	Questionnaire on attitudes	Cross-sectional	Class % white; school % white		SES; individual and Class	+ / 0	Yes	Blacks choose whites significantly more as % white of class rises; early school desegregation has positive effect for whites but not for blacks
McWhirt (1967)	38/38 white, 38/38 black; grade 10; South	Semantic differential; difference in white ratings to white and black	Four-celled	8-month change: desegregated versus segregated	1 year	Sex, age, SES, IQ, aspiration, family size	− / +	Yes	Blacks become more tolerant, whites less tolerant; black girls and white boys become more pro-white than black boys and white girls
Orost (1971)	49 white; kindergarten; New Jersey	Trager and Yarrow's Oral Social Episodes Test	Cross-sectional	A: all-white school; B: integrated school and months; all-white neighborhood; C: integrated school and neighborhood	A few months; voluntary	No	+	Yes	Group A significantly more prejudiced than group C; group B in between; group C showed more stereotypes than B

Chart A-8. *School desegregation and interracial attitudes of white and black pupils (Contd.)*

Study	Sample (N; Grade, Place)	Design					Outcome				Remarks
		Instrument	Design	Comparison	Type and Years of Desegregation	Controls	Whites		Blacks		
							Direction	Significant	Direction	Significant	
Porter (1971)	76/99 white, 91/93 black; preschool, age 3-4; Boston, Mass.	Doll play; interview	Cross-sectional	Desegregated versus segregated in 4 preschools	1-2 years; voluntary	Sex, SES, skin color	± / –	No	± / –	Yes	White boys choose brown dolls more in desegregated schools; white girls choose brown dolls more in segregated school; blacks (light) choose white dolls more in desegregated school; blacks (dark) choose white dolls more in segregated schools
Singer (1966)	60/30 white; 48/48 black; grade 5; northern metropolis	Questionnaire on attitudes; Bogardus Social Distance Scale	Cross-sectional	Desegregated versus segregated	2 years; neighborhood	IQ, SES	+ / –	Yes	+ / 0	Yes	In general, high exposure children of both races significantly more tolerant; intelligent segregated whites tended to be more tolerant, intelligent integrated blacks less tolerant, especially girls

Author	Sample	Measure	Design	Comparison	Controls				Results
Springer (1950)	173 oriental, 34 part oriental, 80 nonoriental, gr K-1, ages 3-6; Honolulu, Hawaii	Picture sort	Cross-sectional	Desegregated oriental versus segregated oriental	No				Both desegregated and segregated chose oriental pictures more often than nonoriental pictures; desegregated orientals gave hair color less frequently and skin color more frequently as reason
Taylor (1967)	17/21/52 white 15/21/22 black; grades 6-7; Maryland and Delaware	Self-social symbols task on attitudes	Four-celled	Early desegregated versus first year desegregated versus segregated	No	–	Yes	–	Desegregated whites and blacks increased significantly in identification with friends and reduced the size of groups in which they included themselves, i.e., increased social isolation
U.S. Commission on Civil Rights (1967)	Over 7500 white and black from EEOS data; grade 9 and 12; Metropolitan Northease	Questionnaire on attitudes	Cross-sectional	Class % white; last year and number of years desegregated	Individual and school level of parents' education	+	Yes	+	Preference for desegregated school and friends of other race positively related to number of years desegregated and class % white

Chart A-8. School desegregation and interracial attitudes of white and black pupils (Concl.)

Study	Sample (N; Grade; Place)	Instrument	Design	Comparison	Type and Years of Desegregation	Controls	Outcome Whites Direction	Whites Significant	Blacks Direction	Blacks Significant	Remarks
Useem (1971)	1042 white (METCO); grade 10 in 8 H.S.; suburban Boston, Mass.	Questionnaire on attitudes	Cross-sectional	Prior contact and contact in school activities	1-3 years; voluntary for blacks	SES, Sex, GPA, ability group	+	Yes			The greater the student's prior equal-status contact with blacks and the greater the contact in school activities, the more positive his attitude toward METCO
Webster (1961)	60 white and 44 black; grade 7 Berkeley, Cal.	Questionnaire on attitudes	Four-celled	1-year change: desegregated versus segregated	1 year; system-wide mandatory	No (SES was similar)	–	Yes	+	Yes	Desegregated whites less accepting than segregated whites and decline further over the year (significantly); desegregated blacks more accepting than segregated blacks and become more accepting (significantly) over the year

Chart A-9. School desegregation and interracial behavior of white and black pupils

| | | | Design | | | | Outcome | | | | |
| | | | | | | | Whites | | Blacks | | |
Study	Sample (N; Grade; Place)	Instrument	Design	Comparison	Type and Years of Desegregation	Controls	Direction	Significant	Direction	Significant	Remarks
Aaronson and Noble (1966)	1000 white, 200 black; grades 2-12; West Hartford, Conn.	Sociometric; observed seating	Longitudinal	Change over summer	6 weeks; voluntary for blacks	No	0		0		Tendency toward increased cross racial choosing; observed seating more interracial at elementary level, less at H.S.
Criswell (1939)	950 white and black; grades K-9; New York City	Sociometric	Cross-sectional	School % white	Neighborhood	Sex	+ −		−		Blacks and white boys more in-group in minority situations, white girls in majority situations
Deutsch-berger (1946)	309/179 white males; ages 9-16; New York and Pittsburgh	Questioned orally on friendships	Four-celled	Neighborhood % white	6 months; changing neighborhood	Sex, SES	−	Yes			Significant decrease in friendship range for changing neighborhood; slight gain (not significant) for stable neighborhood
Fox (1966)	941 white and black; grades 3-6; New York City	Sociometric	Cross-sectional	Class % white in open enrollment classrooms	1 year; voluntary for blacks	No	0		−	a	As % of open enrollment in class rises, blacks choose more whites as good friends; no difference by class % white for whites

Chart A-9. School desegregation and interracial behavior of white and black pupils (Contd.)

Study	Sample (N; Grade; Place)	Instrument	Design	Comparison	Type and Years of Desegregation	Controls	Whites Direction	Whites Signif icant	Blacks Direction	Blacks Signif icant	Remarks
Gottlieb and Ten-Houten (1965)	2516 white/2662 black; high school; mid-west inner city	Sociometric; questionnaire on friendship	Cross-sectional	School A: 4% black; B: 47% black; C: 99% black	Neighborhood	Sex	+ / −	a	+ / −	a	For black boys and white girls, self-preference rises with % own group; for white boys and black girls self-preference declines with % own group
Justman (1968)	277 classes, white and black; grades 3-6; New York City	Sociometric	Cross-sectional	Class % white in open enrollment classrooms	1 year; voluntary for blacks	No	+	a	+	a	Cross-racial acceptance increases with % other group
Kaplan and Matkom (1967)	284 white/88 black; grades 2-8; north	Sociometric	Cross sectional	Class % white (14 classes in school 24% black)		IQ	0		0		No discernible effects of class-room racial composition
Koslin et al. (1972)	95/158 white and black; grade 3; large	Sociometric; classroom preference	Cross-sectional	Classroom racial balance versus imbalance		Middle-class school; school %	+	No	+	No	High level of racial polarization but less in balanced class-rooms; students have more

Study	Sample	Test; people test	Design	Within grade	Black	Contact	Result	Result	Findings
Kupferer (1954)	45 white and black girls; high school; Connecticut	Sociometric	Longitudinal	Change over semester	Sex	1 semester; integrated hockey team	0	0	No change in friendship choice from playing field hockey on integrated teams
Lewis (1971)	497 white/ 412 black; grade 6; Boston, Mass.	Sociometric	Cross-sectional	Class % white	Sex, SES, class SES, GPA	1-6 years; voluntary for blacks	0	0 +	Class % white positively and significantly related to own group preference for black girls but not for other race/ sex groups
Lundberg and Dickson (1952)	3000 in 2 multiethnic H.S.; California	Sociometric	Cross-sectional	School % own group	Sex	Neighborhood	− No	− No	All ethnic groups more ethnocentric in schools with small % own group
Patchen and Davidson (1973)	2300 white, 2000 black; 12 H.S. (0-99% white); Indianapolis, Ind.	Questionnaire on attitudes and behavior	Cross-sectional	% white of present H.S. and earlier elementary schools	None	Varied	+	+	The greater the % black the more friendly contacts whites report and the less negative behavior blacks report; the more interracial contact in elementary schools the more friendly is contact in H.S.

other race choices in balanced classrooms, but not significantly

Chart A-9. School desegregation and interracial behavior of white and black pupils (Concl.)

Study	Sample (N; Grade, Place)	Instrument	Design	Comparison	Type and Years of Desegregation	Controls	Whites Direction	Whites Signif-icant	Blacks Direction	Blacks Signif-icant	Remarks
Schmuck and Luszki (1969)	63 white, 63 black; 8 elementary classrooms; small mid-western communities	Sociometric; self-perception of popularity	Cross-sectional	Class % white: <20%/60-75%/75-100%	White and black matched on SES; none for black/black comparison	0		0			Little difference by class % white in sociometric rating or feeling of being liked by peers
St. John (1964)	230 black; grade 11 in 2 H.S.; New Haven, Conn.	Sociometric	Cross-sectional	Elementary school % white	2-11 years; neighborhood	Sex, SES, curriculum			+ 0	Yes	Early desegregation related positively to black popularity with white but not to black friendliness to white, except in college division
St. John (1969)	1388 white and black; grade 9 in 8 H.S.; Pittsburgh, Pa.	Sociometric	Cross-sectional	Current school % white (9) and previous school % white (1-9)	1-3 years; 1-9 years; neighborhood	No; SES	−		+ −	Yes	The greater the % other group in the school the higher the % of choices to that group, but the greater the own group preference. For blacks,

Study	Sample	Measure	Design	Variable	Controls		Significant?		Findings
St. John and Lewis (1973)	497 white, 412 black; grade 6 in 18 schools (0-94% white); Boston, Mass.	Sociometric	Cross-sectional	Class % white (6) and school % white (1-6)	IQ, SES, class SES	0 +	Yes	0 +	Class % white positively related to friendliness of white boys and black girls only; early desegregation negatively related to friendliness of black boys
Smith (1969)	450 white/795 black (approx); grades 8-12; East	Sociometric	Cross-sectional	% white of eighth-grade school	No	+	Yes	—[a]	Cross-racial friendship most likely for studenst who spent grade 8 in an integrated school
Walker (1968)	46/46 black; grades 7 and 8; Dade County, Fla.	Sociometric; Syracuse Scale of Social Relations	Four-celled	2-year change: desegregated versus segregated	SES (measured through home interviews)	+ −	Yes	+	Popularity of blacks with whites depended on sex and SES; girls lost and boys gained status – the lower class in first year, the middle class in second year; popularity of blacks with whites declined
Yarrow, Campbell, and Yarrow (1958)	65 whites/61 blacks; ages 8-13; inter-racial camp	Sociometric; choice of cabin mates; interviews	Longitudinal	Change over 2 weeks	Sex; alike in SES (low) and residence	+	Yes	−	White and black preference for white cabin mates dropped significantly over 2 weeks

Bibliography

Aberdeen, Frank D. "Adjustment to Desegregation: A Description of Some Differences among Negro Elementary School Pupils," unpublished doctoral dissertation, University of Michigan, 1969.

Allport, Gordon W. *The Nature of Prejudice,* Cambridge, Mass. Addison-Wesley, 1954

Altshuler, Alan A. *Community Control: The Black Demand for Participation in Large American Cities,* New York, Western, 1970.

Anderson, Louis V. *The Effect of Desegregation on the Achievement and Personality Patterns of Negro Children,* unpublished doctoral dissertation, George Peabody College for Teachers, University Microfilm 66–11, 237, 1966.

Archibald, David K. "Report on Change in Academic Achievement for a Sample of Elementary School Children: Progress report on METCO," Roxbury, Mass., 1967. (mimeographed)

Arendt, Hannah. "Reflections on Little Rock," *Dissent* (Winter 1959), 45–55.

Arendt, Hannah. "A Reply to Critics," *Dissent* (Spring 1959), 179–181.

Armor, David, "The Racial Composition of Schools and College Aspirations of Negro Students," in Appendix C2 to *Racial*

Isolation in the Public Schools, U. S. Commission on Civil Rights, Washington, D.C., 1967.

Armor, David J. "The Evidence on Busing," *The Public Interest,* **28** (Summer 1972), 90–126.(a)

Armor, David J. "School and Family Effects on Black and White Achievement: A Reexamination of the USOE Data," in Frederick Mosteller and Daniel P. Moynihan (eds.), *On Equality of Educational Opportunity,* New York, Random House, 1972, 168–229.(b)

Armstrong, C. P., and Gregor, A. James, "Integrated Schools and Negro Character Development: Some Considerations of the Possible Effects," *Psychiatry,* **27** (February 1964), 69–72.

Aronson, Sidney, and Noble, John. "Urban-Suburban School Mixing: A Feasibility Study", West Hartford Board of Education, 1966. (mimeographed)

Atkinson, John W. *An Introduction to Motivation,* Princeton, N.J., Van Nostrand, 1964.

Ausubel, David P. and Ausubel, Pearl. "Ego Development among Segregated Negro Children," in A. Harry Passow (ed.), *Education in Depressed Areas,* New York, Bureau of Publications, Teachers College, Columbia University, 1963, 109–141.

Bachman, Jerald G., *Youth in Transition,* Vol. 2, Ann Arbor, Mich., Institute for Social Research, University of Michigan, 1970.

Bailey, Stephen K. *Disruption in Urban Public Secondary Schools,* Washington, D.C., National Association of Secondary School Principals, 1970.

Banks, Ronald, and Di Pasquale, Mary E. "A Study of the Educational Effectiveness of Integration," Buffalo, N. Y., Buffalo Public Schools, January 1969.

Barber, Ralph W. *The Effects of Open Enrollment on Anti-Negro and Anti-White Prejudices among Junior High Students in Rochester, New York,* unpublished doctoral dissertation, University of Rochester, 1968.

Bartel, Helmut W., Bartel, Nettie R. and Grill, J. Jeffrey, "A Sociometric View of Some Integrated Open Classrooms. *Journal of Social Issues,* **29** (No. 4) (1973), 159–173.

Baskin, Jane A., et al. "Race Related Civil Disorders 1967–69." Lemberg Center for the Study of Violence, Brandeis University, Report Number 1, 1971.

Becker, Howard S. "Social Class Variations in the Teacher-Pupil Relationship," *Journal of Educational Sociology,* **25** (April 1952), 451–465.

Beker, Jerome. "A Study of Integration in Racially Imbalanced Urban Public Schools," Syracuse University Youth Development Center, Final Report, May 1967. (mimeographed)

Bernard, Viola. "School Desegregation: Some Psychiatric Implications," *Psychiatry,* **21** (1958), 149–158.

Bickel, Alexander M. *The Supreme Court and the Idea of Progress,* New York, Harper and Row, 1970.

Bienvenue, Millard J., Sr. *Effects of School Integration on the Self Concept and Anxiety of Lower Class Negro Adolescent Males,* unpublished doctoral dissertation, Florida State University, 1968.

Binderman, Murray B. "The Failure of Freedom of Choice: Decision-Making in a Southern Black Community," *Social Forces,* **50** (June 1972), 487–498.

Bird, Charles, Monachesi, Elio D., and Burdick, Harvey. "Studies of Group Tension. The Effect of Parental Discouragement of Play Activities upon the Attitudes of White Children towards Negroes," *Child Development,* **23** (December 1952), 295–306.

Bird, Charles, Monachesi, Elio D. and Burdick, Harvey. "Infiltration and the Attitudes of White and Negro Parents and Children," *Journal of Abnormal and Social Psychology,* **47** (1952), 688–699.

Blake, Ekias, Jr. *A Comparison of Intraracial and Interracial Levels of Aspirations,* unpublished doctoral dissertation, University of Illinois, 1960.

Blalock, Hubert M., Jr. *Toward a Theory of Minority-Group Relations,* New York, Wiley, 1967.

Boland, Walter R., et al. "De Facto School Segregation and the Student: A Study of the Schools in Connecticut's Five Major Cities," Institute of Urban Research, University of Connecticut, December 1968. (mimeographed)

Bowles, Samuel, and Levin, Henry M. "The Determinants of Scholastic Achievement: An Appraisal of Some Recent Evidence." *The Journal of Human Resources,* **3** (Winter 1968), 3–24.

Brink, William, and Harris, Louis. *The Negro Revolution in America,* New York, Simon and Schuster, 1964.

√ Bronfenbrenner, Urie. "The Psychological Costs of Quality and Equality in Education," *Child Development,* **38** (December 1967), 909–925.

Brookover, Wilbur B., et al. *Self-concept of Ability and School Achievement,* Michigan State University, College of Education, Cooperative Research, Project No. 1636, ER 31, 1965. (mimeographed)

Brown v. Board of Education. 347 U.S. 483, May 17, 1954.

Bryant, James Chester. *Some Effects of Racial Integration of High School Students on Standardized Achievement Test Scores: Teacher Grades and Drop-Out Rates in Angleton, Texas,* unpublished doctoral dissertation, University of Houston, 1968.

Bullough, Bonnie. "Alienation in the Ghetto," *American Journal of Sociology,* **72** (March 1967), 469–478.

Cagle, Laurence T., and Beker, Jerome. "Social Characteristics and Educational Aspirations of Northern Lower-Class Predominantly Negro Parents Who Accepted and Declined a School Integration Opportunity," *Journal of Negro Education,* **37** (1968), 406–417.

Campbell, Angus, and Schuman, Howard S. *Racial Attitudes in Fifteen American Cities: Supplemental Studies for the National Advisory Commission on Civil Disorders,* New York, Praeger, 1968.

Campbell, Donald T., and Stanley, Julian C. "Experimental and Quasi-Experimental Designs for Research on Teaching," in N. L. Gage (ed.), *Handbook of Research on Teaching,* Chicago, Rand McNally, 1963, 171–246.

Campbell, Ernest Q. *The Attitude Effects of Educational Desegregation in a Southern Community,* unpublished doctoral dissertation, Vanderbilt University, 1956.

√ Carithers, Martha W. "School Desegregation and Racial Cleavage, 1954–1970: A Review of the Literature," *Journal of Social Issues,* **26** (Autumn 1970), 25–47.

Carmichael, Stokely, and Hamilton, Charles V. *Black Power,* New York, Vintage Books, 1967.

Carrigan, Patricia M. "School Desegregation via Compulsory Pupil Transfer: Early Effects on Elementary School Children," Ann Arbor, Michigan, Public Schools, September 1969.

Center for the Study of Public Policy. *Education Vouchers: A Report on Financing Elementary Education by Grants to Parents.* Cambridge, Mass., December, 1970.

Chesler, Mark A., and Segal, Phyllis. *Characteristics of Negro Students Attending Previously All-White Schools in the Deep South.* Institute for Social Research, University of Michigan, September 1967.

Cicourel, Aaron V., and Kitsuse, John I. *The Educational Decision Makers,* Indianapolis, Bobbs Merrill, 1963.

Clark, Kenneth B. *Dark Ghetto: Dilemmas of Social Power,* New York, Harper and Row, 1965.

Clark, Kenneth B. *Prejudice and Your Child,* Boston, Beacon Press, 1955.

√ Clark, Kenneth B. "Just Teach Them to Read," *The New York Times Magazine,* March 18, 1973, 14ff.

Clinchy, Evans, et al. "Springfield Schools in the Seventies," Boston, Mass. Educational Planning Associates, Inc., 1972.

Clinton, Ronald R. *A Study of the Improvement in Achievement of Basic Skills of Children Bused from Urban to Suburban School Environments,* unpublished masters thesis, Southern Connecticut State College, 1969.

Cohen, Albert K. *Delinquent Boys: The Culture of the Gang,* Glencoe, Ill., Free Press, 1955.

Cohen, David K., Pettigrew, Thomas F., and Riley, Robert T. "Race and the Outcomes of Schooling," in Frederick Mosteller and Daniel P. Moynihan (eds.), *On Equality of Educational Opportunity,* New York, Random House, 1972.

Cohen, Elizabeth, et al. "Expectation Training I: Altering the Effects of a Racial Status Characteristic," Technical Report No. 2, Stanford University, School of Education, 1970.

Coleman, A. Lee. "Social Scientists' Predictions about Desegregation, 1950–1955," *Social Forces,* **38** (1960), 258–262.

Coleman, James S. *The Adolescent Society,* Glencoe: Free Press, 1961.

Coleman, James S., et al. *Equality of Educational Opportunity.* Washington, D.C., U.S. Department of Health, Education and Welfare, Office of Education, 1966.

Coles, Robert. *Children of Crisis: A Study of Courage and Fear,* Boston, Little, Brown, 1967.

√ Coles, Robert. "Northern Children Under Desegregation," *Psychiatry,* **31** (February 1968), 1–15.

Coles, Robert. *The South Goes North,* Boston, Little, Brown, 1971.

Conant, James B. *Slums and Suburbs: A Commentary on Schools in Metropolitan Areas,* New York, McGraw-Hill, 1961.

Cooley, Charles Horton. *Human Nature and the Social Order,* New York, Free Press, 1902.

Cottle, Thomas. "The Integration of Harry Benjamin," *New York Times Magazine,* April 23, 1972, 15ff.

Crain, Robert. "School Integration and the Academic Achievement of Negroes," *Sociology of Education,* **44** (Winter 1971), 1–26.

Crain, Robert L. *The Politics of School Desegregation,* Chicago, Aldine, 1968.

Criswell, Joan H. "A Sociometric Study of Racial Cleavage in the Classroom," *Archives of Psychology* (January 1939).

Crockett, Harry J. "A Study of Some Factors Affecting the Decision of Negro High School Students to Enroll in Previously All-White High Schools, St. Louis, 1955," *Social Forces,* **35** (May 1957), 351–356.

Crooks, Roland C. "The Effects of an Interracial Pre-School Program upon Racial Preferences, Knowledge of Racial Differences and Racial Identification," *Journal of Social Issues,* **26** (Autumn 1970), 137–144.

Crowley, Mary R. "Cincinnati's Experiment in Negro Education: A Comparative Study of the Segregated and Mixed School," *Journal of Negro Education,* **1** (April 1932), 25–33.

Curtis, Byron William. *The Effects of Segregation on the Vocational Aspirations of Negro Students,* unpublished doctoral dissertation, University of Miami, 1968.

Dambacher, Arthur D. "Comparison of Achievement Test Scores made by Berkeley Elementary Students Pre and Post Integration Eras, 1967–1970," Berkeley California Unified School District, July 16, 1971. (mimeographed)

Danahy, Ann Hechter. "A Study of the Effects of Bussing on the Achievement, Attendance, Attitudes, and Social Choices of Negro Inner-City Children," unpublished doctoral dissertation, University of Minnesota, 1971.

Davidson, Helen H., and Lang, Gerhard. "Children's Perceptions of their Teachers' Feelings toward them Related to Self-perception, School Achievement and Behavior," *Journal of Experimental Education,* **29(2),** (1960), 107–118.

Davis, James A. "The Campus as a Frog Pond: An Application of the Theory of Relative Deprivation to Career Decisions of College Men," *American Journal of Sociology,* **72** (July 1966), 17–31.

Dean, John P., and Rosen, Alex. *A Manual of Intergroup Relations,* Chicago, University of Chicago Press, 1955.

Denmark, Florence L. "The Effects of Integration on Academic Achievement and Self-Concept," *Integrated Education,* **8** (May-June 1970), 34–42.

Denmark, Florence L. and Guttentag, Marcia. "Effect of Integrated and Non-Integrated Programs on Cognitive Change in Pre-School Children," *Perceptual and Motor Skills,* **29** (October 1969), 375–380.

Dentler, Robert A. "Barriers to Northern School Desegregation," *Daedalus,* **95** (Winter 1966), 45–63.

Dentler, Robert A., and Elkins, Constance. "Intergroup Attitudes, Academic Performance, and Racial Composition," in Robert A. Dentler, Bernard Mackler, and Mary Ellen Warshauer (eds.), *The Urban R's,* New York, Praeger, 1967.

Deutschberger, Paul. "Interaction Patterns in Changing Neighborhoods: New York and Pittsburgh," *Sociometry,* **9** (November 1946), 303–315.

Deutscher, Max, and Chein, Isidor. "The Psychological Effects of Enforced Segregation: A Survey of Social Science Opinion," *Journal of Psychology,* **26** (October 1948), 259–287.

Dimond, Paul R. "Segregation, Northern Style," *Inequality in Education,* **9** (August 1971). (Harvard University, Center for Law and Education).

✓ Dorr, Robin. "Ordeal by Desegregation," *Integrated Education: A Report on Race and Schools,* **10** (July/August, 1972), 34–39.

Downs, Anthony. "Alternative Futures for the American Ghetto," *Daedalus: The Conscience of the City,* **97** (Fall 1968), 1331–1378.

Dressler, Frank J. "Study of Achievement in Reading of Pupils Transferred from Schools 15 and 37 to Peripheral Schools to Eliminate Overcrowding, to Abandon an Obsolete School, and to Achieve a more Desirable Racial Balance in City Schools," Buffalo Public Schools, Division of Curriculum Evaluation and Development, March 1967. (mimeographed)

Ehrlich, Howard J. *The Social Psychology of Prejudice, New York, Wiley, 1972.*

Entin, David H. "The Black Burden in Desegregation," *Integrated Education: A Report on Race and Schools,* **10** (July/August 1972), 3–19.

Evans, Charles Lee. *The Immediate Effects of Classroom Integration on the Academic Progress, Self-Concept and Racial Attitudes of Negro Elementary Children,* unpublished doctoral dissertation, North Texas State University, 1969.

Falk, William W., Cosby, Arthur G. and Wright, David. "The Effects of Racial Desegregation on High School Youth's Educational Projections: A Quasi-Experimental Study," Texas A & M University, paper presented at Rural Sociological Society Meeting, August 25, 1973.

Fauman, S. J. "Housing Discrimination, Changing Neighborhoods and Public Schools," *Journal of Social Issues,* **13(4)** (1957), 21–30.

Feldman, Kenneth A. "Using the Work of Others: Some Observations on Reviewing and Integrating," *Sociology of Education,* **44** (Winter 1971), 86–102.

Fisher, James E. *An Exploration of the Effect of Desegregation on the Educational Plans of Negro and White Boys,* unpublished doctoral dissertation. Oklahoma State University, 1970.

Fishman, Joshua A. "Childhood Indoctrination for Minority Group Membership," *Daedalus,* **90** (Spring 1961), 329–349.

Fishman, Joshua A., et al. "Guidelines for Testing Minority Group Children," *Journal of Social Issues,* **20,** (April 1964), 129–145.

Fortenberry, James H. *The Achievement of Negro Pupils in Mixed and Non-Mixed Schools,* unpublished doctoral dissertation, University of Oklahoma, University Microfilm No. 59-5492, 1959.

Fox, David J. "Free Choice Open Enrollment—Elementary Schools," New York, Center for Urban Education, August 1966. (mimeographed)

Fox, David J. "Evaluation of the New York City Title I Educational Projects 1966–1967: Expansion of the Free Choice Open Enrollment Program," New York, Center for the Urban Education, September 1967. (mimeographed)

Fox, David J., et al. "Services to Children in Open Enrollment Receiving Schools: Evaluation of ESEA Title I Projects in New York City, 1967–1968," New York, Center for Urban Education, November 1968. (mimeographed)

Frary, Robert B., and Goolsby, Thomas M., Jr. "Achievement of Integrated and Segregated Negro and White First Graders in a Southern City," *Integrated Education,* **8** (July/August 1970), 48–52.

Freeman, Howard E., et al. "Color Gradation and Attitudes among Middle Class Negroes," *American Sociological Review,* **31** (June 1966), 365–374.

Frelow, Robert D. *A Comparative Study of Resource Allocation: Compensatory Education and School Desegregation,* Unpublished doctoral dissertation, University of California, Berkeley, 1971.

Frenkel-Brunswick, Else, and Havel, Jean. "Prejudice in the Interviews of Children: Attitudes towards Minority Groups," *Journal of Genetic Psychology,* **82** (1953), 91–136.

Gardner, Burleigh B., et al. "The Effect of Busing Black Ghetto Children into White Suburban Schools," July 1970 (ERIC ED 048 389).

√ Garrett, Henry E. *How Classroom Desegregation Will Work,* Richmond, Patrick Henry Press, 1966.

Garth, Charles E. *Self-Concept of Negro Students Who Transferred and Did Not Transfer to Formerly All-White High Schools.* unpublished doctoral dissertation, University of Kentucky, 1969.

Gerard, Harold B., and Miller, Norman. "Factors Contributing to Adjustment and Achievement in Racially Desegregated Public Schools," Department of Psychology, University of California, Los Angeles, 1971. (mimeographed)

Glazer, Nathan. "Is Busing Necessary?," *Commentary,* **53** (March 1972), 39–52.

Goffman, Erwin G. *Stigma: Notes on the Management of Spoiled Identity,* Englewood Cliffs, N.J., Prentice-Hall, 1963.

Goldman, Peter. *Report from Black America,* New York, Simon and Schuster, 1970.

Goodman, Walter. "Busing for Integration is Working Well in Central 7 School District—Knock Wood," *The New York Times Magazine,* April 9, 1972, 31ff.

Gordon, Edmund W., and Wilkerson, Doxey A. "A Critique of Compensatory Education," in *Compensatory Education for the Disadvantaged,* New York, College Entrance Examination Board, 1966.

Gordon, Leonard. *An Acculturation Analysis of Negro and White High School Students: The Effects on Social and Academic Behavior of Initial Close Interracial Association at the Secondary School Level,* unpublished doctoral dissertation, Wayne State University, 1966.

Gottlieb, David, and TenHouten, Warren D. "Racial Composition and the Social Systems of Three High Schools," *Journal of Marriage and the Family,* **27** (May 1965), 204–212.

Graves, Marian F., and Bedell, Frederick D. "A Three-Year Evaluation of the White Plains Racial Balance Plan," White Plains, N. Y., Board of Education, October 16, 1967. (mimeographed)

Greeley, Andrew M., and Sheatsley, Paul B. "Attitudes toward Racial Integration," *Scientific American,* **225** (December 1971), 13–19.

Grier, William H., and Cobbs, Price M. *Black Rage,* New York, Basic Books, 1968.

Griffin, J. L. *The Effects of Integration on Academic Aptitude, Classroom Achievement, Self-Concept and Attitudes toward the School Environment of a Selected Group of Negro Students in Tulsa, Oklahoma,* unpublished doctoral dissertation, University of Tulsa, 1969.

Gross, Neal, Mason, Ward S., and McEachern, Alexander W. *Explorations in Role Analysis: Studies of the School Superintendency Role,* Wiley, 1958.

Group for the Advancement of Psychiatry. *Psychiatric Aspects of School Desegregation,* Report No. 37, New York, 1957.

Gurin, Patricia, et al. "Internal-External Control in the Motivational Dynamics of Negro Youth. *Journal of Social Issues,* **25** (Summer 1969), 29–54.

Guttentag, Marcia. "Children in Harlem's Community Controlled Schools," *Journal of Social Issues,* **28(4)** (1972), 1–20.

Haggstrom, Warren C. *Self Esteem and Other Characteristics of Residentially Desegregated Negroes,* unpublished doctoral dissertation, University of Michigan, 1962.

Haggstrom, Warren C. "Segregation, Desegregation and Negro Personality," *Integrated Education,* **1** (October/November 1963), 19–23.

Hall, Morrill M., and Gentry, Harold W. "Isolation of Negro Students in Integrated Public Schools," *Journal of Negro Education,* **38** (Spring 1969), 156–161.

Hamilton, Charles V. "Race and Education: A Search for Legitimacy," *Harvard Educational Review,* **38** (Fall 1968), 669–684.

Hamilton, Charles V. "The Nationalist vs. the Integrationist," *The New York Times Magazine,* October 1, 1972, 36 ff.

Handlin, Oscar. "The Goals of Integration," *Daedalus,* **95** (Winter 1966), 268–286.

Hansen, Carl F. "The Scholastic Performances of Negro and White Pupils in the Integrated Public Schools of the District of Columbia," *Harvard Educational Review,* **30** (Summer 1960), 216–236.

Hanusheh, Eric Alan. *The Education of Negroes and Whites,* unpublished doctoral dissertation, Massachusetts Institute of Technology, 1969.

Harootunia, Berj. "Self-Other Relationship of Segregated and Desegregated Ninth Graders," paper presented at the Annual Meeting of the American Educational Research Association, February 1968 (ERIC ED 023 765).

√   Harris, Louis. "Antibusing Attitudes Harden," *The Boston Globe,* April 10, 1972, 4.

Harnett, Rodney T. "Differences in Selected Attitudes and College Orientations between Black Students Attending Traditionally Negro and Traditionally White Institutions," *Sociology of Education,* **43** (Fall 1970), 419–436.

Havighurst, Robert J. "Crisis in Urban Education," in H. J. Walberg and A. T. Kopan (eds.), *Rethinking Urban Education,* San Francisco, Jossey-Bass, 1972, 303–316.

Heller, Barbara R. et al. "Project Concern: Westport, Connecticut Center for Urban Education, New York, N.Y., June 1972.

Heller, Celia Stopnicka. *Ambitions of Mexican Youth: Goals and Means of Mobility of High School Seniors,* unpublished doctoral dissertation, Columbia University, 1964.

Hermalin, Albert I., and Farley, Reynolds. "The Potential for Residential Integration in Cities and Suburbs: Implications for the Busing Controversy," *American Sociological Review* **38** (October 1973), 595–610.

Herman, Barry. "Interracial Attitudes Among 175 Sixth Grade Students," *Curriculum Leadership,* **9** No. 1 (1970), 30–35.

Herman, Barry E. "The Effect of Neighborhood Upon the Attitudes of Negro and White Sixth Grade Children Toward Different Racial Groups," unpublished doctoral dissertation, University of Connecticut, 1967.

Herriott, Robert, E., and St. John, Nancy Hoyt. *Social Class and the Urban School,* New York, Wiley, 1966.

Herzog, Elizabeth. "Social Stereotypes and Social Research," *Journal of Social Issues,* **26** (Summer 1970), 109–125.

Hill, Roscoe, and Feeley, Malcolm eds. *Affirmative School Integration: Efforts to Overcome De Facto Segregation in Urban Schools,* New York, Russell Sage, 1967.

Holden, Anna. *The Bus Stops Here: A Study of Desegregation in Three Cities,* Center for Urban Education, New York, Agathon Press, 1974.

Holland, Florence N. "A Comment on the Segregated Learning Situation as an Insulating Device for the Negro Child," *Psychiatry,* **27** (August 1964), 301–303.

Hope, Richard O. "The Differential Effects of Residential Status on Student Assimilation," in Jerome Beker (ed.), "A Study of Integration in Racially Imbalanced Urban Public Schools," Syracuse University Youth Development Center, May 1967. (mimeographed)

Hsia, Jayjia. "Integration in Evanston, 1967–1971," Educational Testing Service, Princeton, N. J., August 1971. (mimeographed).

Jencks, Christopher. "Busing—The Supreme Court Goes North," *The New York Times Magazine,* November 19, 1972. (a) p. 41ff

Jencks, Christopher S. "The Coleman Report and the Conventional Wisdom," in Frederick Mosteller and Daniel P. Moynihan (eds.), *On Equality of Educational Opportunity,* New York, Random House, 1972. (b)

Jencks, Christopher, and Brown, Marsha. "The Effects of Desegregation on Student Achievement: Some New Evidence from the Equality of Educational Opportunity Survey," Center for Educational Policy Research, Harvard Graduate School of Education, November 1972. (mimeographed)

Jencks, Christopher, et al. *Inequality: A Reassessment of the Effect of Family and Schooling in America,* New York, Basic Books, 1972.

Jessup, Dorothy K. "School Integration and Minority Group Achievement," in Robert A. Dentler, Bernard Mackler, and Mary Ellen Warschauer (eds.), *The Urban R's: Race Relations as the Problem in Urban Education,* New York, Praeger, 1967.

Johnson, Norman J., Wyer, Robert, and Gilbert, Neil. "Quality Education and Integration: An Exploratory Study," *Phylon,* **28** (Fall 1967), 221–229.

Jonsson, Harold. Report of Evaluation of ESEA Title I, Berkeley, California (August 1966). (mimeographed)

Jonsson, Harold A. "Effectiveness of ESEA Title I Activities in the Berkeley Unified School District: A Short Summary of Evaluation for the 1966–1967 Project Year," Berkeley, Calif., 1967. (mimeographed)

Justman, Joseph. "Children's Reactions to Open Enrollment," *The Urban Review,* **3** (November 1968), 32–34.

Kaplan, Henry K., and Matkom, Anthony J. "Peer Status and Intellectual Functioning of Negro School Children," *Psychology in the Schools,* **4** (April 1967), 181–184.

Katz, I., Epps, E. G., and Axelson, L. J. "Effect upon Negro Digit-Symbol Performance of Anticipated Comparison with Whites and with Other Negroes," *Journal of Abnormal and Social Psychology,* **69** (1964), 77–83.

Katz, I., and Greenbaum, C. "Effects of Anxiety, Threat and Racial Environment on Task Performance of Negro College Students," *Journal of Abnormal and Social Psychology,* **66** (1963), 562–567.

Katz, I., Roberts, S. O., and Robinson, J. M. "Effects of Task Difficulty, Race of Administrator and Instructions on Digit-Symbol Performance of Negroes," *Journal of Personality and Social Psychology,* **70** (1965), 53–59.

Katz, Irwin. "Review of Evidence Relating to Effects of Desegregation on the Intellectual Performance of Negroes," *American Psychologist,* **19** (1964), 381–399.

Katz, Irwin. "The Socialization of Academic Motivation in Minority Group Children," in Donald Levine (ed.), *Nebraska Symposium on Motivation, 1967,* Vol. 15, Lincoln, University of Nebraska Press, 1967.

Katz, Irwin. "Factors Influencing Negro Performance in the Desegregated School," in Martin Deutsch, Irwin Katz, and Arthur Jensen (eds.), *Social Class, Race and Psychological Development,* New York, Holt, Rinehart and Winston, 1968.

Katzenmeyer, William Gilbert. *Social Interaction and Differences in Intelligence Test Performance of Negro and White Elementary School Pupils,* unpublished doctoral dissertation, Duke University, 1962.

Kelley, Harold H. "Two Functions of Reference Groups," in Guy E. Swanson, Theodore M. Newcomb, and Eugene L. Hartley (eds.), *Readings in Social Psychology,* New York, Holt Rinehart and Winston, 1952.

Kemper, Theodore D. "Reference Groups, Socialization and Achievement," *American Sociological Review,* **33** (February 1968), 31–45.

King, Charles E., and Mayer, Robert R. "A Pilot Study of the Social and Educational Impact of School Desegregation," September 1971. (mimeographed)

Kirby, David J., et al. *School Desegregation in the North: A Preliminary Report,* The Johns Hopkins University, Center for the Study of Social Organization of Schools, Report No. 86, 1970.

Klein, Robert Stanley. *A Comparative Study of the Academic Achievement of Negro Tenth Grade High School Students Attending Segregated and Recently Integrated Schools in a Metropolitan Area in the South,* unpublished doctoral dissertation, University of South Carolina, 1967.

Knight, James Henry. *The Interpersonal Values and Aspiration Levels of Negro Seniors in Totally Integrated and Totally Segregated Southern High Schools,* unpublished doctoral dissertation, University of North Carolina, 1970.

Koslin, S., Koslin, B. L., and Pargament, R. "Efficacy of School Integration Policies in Reducing Racial Polarization," Riverside Research Institute, 1972. (mimeographed)

Koslin, Sandra, et al. "Classroom Racial Balance and Students' Interracial Attitudes," *Sociology of Education,* **45** (Fall 1972), 386–407.

Kupferer, Harriet J. "An Evaluation of the Integration Potential of a

Physical Education Program," *Journal of Educational Sociology,* **28** (October 1954), 89–96.

Kurokawa, Minako. "Mutual Perceptions of Racial Images: White, Black, and Japanese Americans," *Journal of Social Issues,* **27** (4) (1971), 213–235.

Laird, Mary Alice, and Weeks, Grace. "The Effect of Bussing on Achievement in Reading and Arithmetic in Three Philadelphia Schools," The School District of Philadelphia, Division of Research, December 1966. (mimeographed)

Lammers, Donald M. *Self Concepts of American Indian Adolescents Having Segregated and Desegregated Elementary Backgrounds,* unpublished doctoral dissertation, Syracuse University, 1969.

Laurent, James A. *Effects of Race and Racial Balance of School on Academic Performance,* unpublished doctoral dissertation, University of Oregon, 1969.

Lewis, Charles E., Jr. *School Integration and Occupational Expectations: A Study of North Carolina High School Senior Boys,* unpublished doctoral dissertation, North Carolina State University at Raleigh, 1970.

Lewis, Ralph G. *The Relationship of Classroom Racial Composition to Student Academic Achievement and the Conditioning Effects of Inter-Racial Social Acceptance,* unpublished doctoral dissertation, Harvard Graduate School of Education, 1971.

Lewis, Ralph, and St. John, Nancy. "Contribution of Cross-Racial Friendship to Minority Group Achievement in Desegregated Classrooms, *Sociometry,* **37** (1) (1974) 79–91.

Light, Richard J., and Smith, Paul V. "Accumulating Evidence: Procedures for Resolving Contradictions among Different Research Studies," *Harvard Educational Review,* **41** (November 1971), 429–471.

Lindsay, Carl A., and Gottlieb, David. "High School Racial Composition and Educational Aspiration," paper presented at American Sociological Association meeting, 1969.

Lindzey, Gardner, and Borgatta, Edgar F. "Sociometric Measurement," in Gardner Lindzey (ed.), *Handbook of Social Psychology,* Cambridge, Mass., Addison-Wesley, 1954, 405–448.

Lockwood, Jane Durand. *An Examination of Scholastic Achievement, Attitudes and Home Background Factors of 6th Grade Negro Students in Balanced and Unbalanced Schools,* unpublished doctoral dissertation, University of Michigan, 1966.

Lombardi, Donald N. *Factors Affecting Changes in Attitudes toward Negroes among High School Students,* unpublished doctoral dissertation, Fordham University, 1962.

Long, David. *Educational Performance in Integrated and Segregated Elementary Schools,* unpublished doctoral dissertation, Yeshiva University, 1968.

Luchterhand, Elmer, and Weller, Leonard. "Social Class and the Desegregation Movement: A Study of Parents' Decisions in a Negro Ghetto," *Social Problems,* **13** (Summer 1965), 83–88.

Lundberg, George and Dickson, Lenore. "Inter ethnic Relations in a High School Population," *American Journal of Sociology,* **58** (July 1952), 1–10.

Lundberg, George A., and Dickson, Lenore. "Selective Association among Ethnic Groups in a High School Population," *American Sociological Review,* **17** (February 1952), 23–35.

Lynn, Lawrence E., Jr. *The Effectiveness of Compensatory Education: Summary and Review of the Evidence,* U.S. Department of Health, Education and Welfare, April 1972.

Mack, Raymond W. *Our Children's Burden,* New York, Random House, 1968.

Mahan, T. W. "Project Concern—1966–68: A Report on the Effectiveness of Suburban School Placement for Inner-City Youth," Hartford, Connecticut, Board of Education, August 1968.

Mahan, Thomas W., and Mahan, Alice M. "The Impact of Schools on Learning: Inner City Children in Suburban Schools," *Journal of School Psychology,* **9** (1) (1971), 1–11.

Marascuilo, Leonard A., and Dagenais, F. "The Meaning of the Word 'Integration' to Seniors in a Multi-Racial High School," Far West Laboratory for Educational Research and Development, University of California, Berkeley, 1972.

MARC Busing Task Force, "Fact Book on Pupil Transportation," Metropolitan Applied Research Center, New York, 1972.

Marcum, Roger Brasel. *An Exploration of the First Year Effects of Racial Integration of the Elementary Schools in a Unit School District,* unpublished doctoral dissertation, University of Illinois, 1968.

Marx, Gary T. *Protest and Prejudice: A Study of Belief in the Black Community,* New York, Harper and Row, 1967.

Matzen, Stanley Paul. *The Relationship between Racial Composition and Scholastic Achievement in Elementary School Classrooms,* unpublished doctoral dissertation, Stanford University, 1965.

Mayer, Robert R., et al. *The Impact of School Desegregation in a Southern City,* Boston, Heath, 1974.

Mayeske, G., et al. *A Study of Our Nation's Schools,* Washington, D.C., U.S. Department of Health, Education and Welfare, 1972.

Mayeske, George, et al. "Item Response Analyses of the Educational Survey Student Questionnaires," Technical Note Number 64, April 1968, U.S. Office of Education.

Maynor, Waltz. *Academic Performance and School Integration: A Multi-Ethnic Analysis,* unpublished doctoral dissertation, Duke University, 1970.

McCauley, Patrick, and Ball, Edward D., eds. *Southern Schools: Progress and Problems.* Nashville, Tenn., Southern Education Reporting Service, 1959.

McCullough, James S. "Academic Achievement under School Desegregation in a Southern City," University of North Carolina, Chapel Hill Department of City and Regional Planning, January 1972. (mimeographed)

McPartland, James. *The Segregated Student in Desegregated Schools: Sources of Influence on Negro Secondary Students,* Center for the Study of Social Organization of Schools, Baltimore, Md. The Johns Hopkins University, Report No. 21, 1968.

McWhirt, Ronald A. *The Effects of Desegregation on Prejudice, Academic Aspiration and The Self-Concept of Tenth Grade Students,* unpublished doctoral dissertation, University of South Carolina, 1967.

Mead, George H. *Mind, Self, and Society,* Chicago, University of Chicago Press, 1934.

Meketon, Betty F. *The Effects of Integration upon the Negro Child's Response to Various Tasks and upon His Level of Self-Esteem,* unpublished doctoral dissertation, University of Kentucky, 1966.

Merton, Robert K. *Social Theory and Social Structure,* Glencoe, Free Press, 1957.

Metzger, L. Paul. "American Sociology and Black Assimilation: Conflicting Perspectives," *American Journal of Sociology,* **76** (January 1971), 627–647.

Milner, Esther. "Some Hypotheses Concerning the Influence of Segregation on Negro Personality Development," *Psychiatry,* **16** (August 1953), 291–297.

Moorefield, Thomas. *The Bussing of Minority Group Children in a Big City School System,* unpublished doctoral dissertation, University of Chicago, 1967.

Moreno, Jacob, J. *Who Shall Survive?,* Boston, Beacon House, 1953, Revised Edition

Mosher, D. L., and Scodel, A. "Relationships between Ethnocentrism in Children and the Ethnocentrism and Authoritarian Rearing Practices of Their Mothers," *Child Development,* **31** (1960), 369–376.

Mosteller, Frederick, and Moynihan, Daniel P. *On Equality of Educational Opportunity,* New York, Random House, 1972.

Myrdal, Gunnar. *An American Dilemma,* New York, Harper and Brothers, 1944.

National Academy of Sciences. *Freedom of Choice in Housing: Opportunities and Constraints,* Social Science Panel of Advisory Committee to the Department of Housing and Urban Development, Washington, D.C., 1972.

National Advisory Commission on Civil Disorders, *Report to the Commission,* New York, Bantam Books, 1968.

New York Times, "Black Convention Eases Busing and Israeli Stands," May 20, 1972.

Office of Civil Rights, U.S. Department of Health, Education and Welfare, Tables released January, 1971, reproduced in *Integrated Education,* **9** (March/April 1971), 40–43.

O'Reilly, Robert P., ed. *Racial and Social Class Isolation in the Schools,* New York, Praeger, 1970.

Orost, Jean H. "Racial Attitudes among White Kindergarten Children from Three Different Environments," paper presented at American Educational Research Association Meeting, New York, February 1971.

Paige, Jeffery M. "Changing Patterns of Anti-White Attitudes among Blacks," *Journal of Social Issues,* **26** (Autumn 1970), 69–86.

Palmer, James M., Sr. "Resegregation and the Private School Movement," *Integrated Education,* **9** (May/June 1971), 4–10.

Park, Robert Ezra. *Race and Culture,* Glencoe, Ill., Free Press, 1950.

Parsons, Theodore William Jr. *Ethnic Cleavage in a California School,* unpublished doctoral dissertation, Stanford University, 1965.

Patchen, Martin, and Davidson, James D. *Patterns and Determinants of Inter-Racial Interaction in the Indianapolis Public High Schools,* 1973. (mimeographed)

Perry, George A. *A Better Chance: Evaluation of Student Attitudes and Academic Performance, 1964–1972,* Boston, Mass., A Better Chance, 1973.

Pettigrew, Thomas F. *A Profile of the Negro American,* Princeton, N.J., Van Nostrand, 1964.

Pettigrew, Thomas F. "Social Evaluation Theory: Convergences and Applications," in Daniel Levine (ed.), *Nebraska Symposium on Motivation, 1967,* Vol. 15, Lincoln, University of Nebraska Press, 1967, 241–311.

Pettigrew, Thomas F. "The Negro and Education: Problems and Proposals," in Irwin Katz and Patricia Gurin (eds.), *Race and the Social Sciences,* New York, Basic Books, 1969.

Pettigrew, Thomas F. *Racially Separate or Together?,* New York, McGraw-Hill, 1971.

Pettigrew, Thomas F., et al. "Busing: A Review of the Evidence", *Public Interest* (Winter 1973), 88–118.

Pierce, Chester M. "Problems of the Negro Adolescent in the Next Decade," in Eugene Brody (ed.), *Minority Group Adolescents in the U. S.,* Baltimore, Williams & Wilkins, 1968.

Pinderhughes, C. A. "Effects of Ethnic Group Concentration upon Education Process, Personality Formation, and Mental Health," *Journal of National Medical Association,* **56** (1964), 407.

Piven, Francis F., and Cloward, Richard A. "The Case Against Urban Desegregation," *Social Work,* **12** (January 1967), 12–21.

√ Porter, Judith D. R. *Black Child–White Child,* Cambridge, Mass., Harvard University Press, 1971.

Poussaint, Alvin F. Introduction to *What Students Perceive,* a report to the U.S. Commission on Civil Rights, Clearing House Publication, 24 (1970).

Powell, Gloria J., and Fuller, Marielle. "Self-Concept and School Desegregation," *Journal of Orthopsychiatry,* **40** (March 1970), 303–304.

Prichard, Paul N. "Effects of Desegregation on Student Success in the Chapel Hill School," *Integrated Education,* **7** (November/December 1969), 33–38.

Prichard, Paul N. *The Effects of Desegregation on Selected Variables in the Chapel Hill City School System,* unpublished doctoral dissertation, University of North Carolina, 1969.

Proshansky, Harold M. "The Development of Intergroup Attitudes," L. W. Hoffman and M. L. Hoffman (eds.), *In Review of Child Development Research,* New York, Russel Sage, 1966, 2 - 311–371.

Proshansky, Harold, and Newton, Peggy "The Nature and Meaning of Negro Self-Identity," Deutsch, Katz, and Jensen (eds.), *In Social Class, Race, and Psychological Development,* New York, Holt, Rinehart and Winston, 1968, 178–218.

Purl, Mabel C., and Dawson, Judith, A. "The Achievement of Pupils in Desegregated Schools," Riverside, Calif., Riverside Unified School District, March 1971. (mimeographed)

Purl, Mabel C., and Dawson, Judith A. "The Achievement of Students in Primary Grades after Seven Years of Desegregation," Riverside, Calif., Riverside Unified School District, February 1973. (mimeographed)

Ransford, H. Edward "Skin Color, Life Chances and Anti-White Attitudes," *Social Problems,* **18** (Fall 1970), 164–179.

Rentsch, George Jacob. *Open-Enrollment: An Appraisal,* unpublished doctoral dissertation, State University of New York, Buffalo, 1967.

"Replies to Jensen", *Harvard Educational Review,* **39** (Spring 1969), 273–356.

Robertson, William Joseph. *The Effects of Junior High School Segregation Experience on the Achievement Behavior and Academic Motivation of Integrated 10th Grade Students,* unpublished doctoral dissertation, University of Michigan, 1967.

Rochester City School District. *Final Report: A Three-Year Longitudinal Study to Assess a Fifteen-Point Plan to Reduce Racial Isolation and Provide Quality Integrated Education for Elementary Level Pupils,* September 1970.

Rock, William C., et al. "A Report on a Cooperative Program Between a City School District and a Suburban School District," Rochester, N.Y., June 28, 1968.

Rogers, David. *New York City and the Politics of School Desegregation,* Center for Urban Education, July 1968.

Rosenberg, Morris, and Simmons, Roberta G. *Black and White Self-Esteem: The Urban School Child,* Arnold M. and Caroline Rose Monograph Series, American Sociological Association, Washington, D.C., 1971.

Rosenthal, Robert, and Jacobson, Lenore. *Pygmalion in the Classroom,* New York, Holt, Rinehart and Winston, 1968.

Rossell, Christine H., and Crain, Robert L. "Evaluating School Desegregation Statistically" The Johns Hopkins University, Center for Metropolitan Planning and Research, November, 1973. (mimeographed)

Rubin, Lillian B. *Busing and Backlash: White Against White in a*

California School District, Berkeley, University of California Press, 1972.

Runcimen, Hon. Walter G. *Relative Deprivation and Social Justice,* London: Routledge and Keegan Paul, 1966.

Sacramento City Unified School District, *Focus on Reading and Math, 1970–71: A Evaluation Report on a Program of Compensatory Education,* E.S.E.A., Title 1, July 1971.

Saenger, Gerhart. *The First Year of the Open Enrollment Program: A Pilot Study,* Report to the Commission of Intergroup Relations, New York, 1961. (mimeographed)

St. John, Nancy Hoyt. *A Study of the Aspirations of a Selected Group of Negro High School Graduates,* unpublished masters thesis, Brown University, 1958.

St. John, Nancy Hoyt. *The Relation of Racial Segregation in Early Schooling to the Level of Aspiration and Academic Achievement of Negro Students in a Northern High School,* unpublished doctoral dissertation, Harvard University, 1962.

St. John, Nancy Hoyt. "De Facto Segregation and Interracial Association in High School," *Sociology of Education,* **37** (Summer 1964), 326–344.

St. John, Nancy Hoyt. "The Effect of Segregation on the Aspirations of Negro Youth," *Harvard Educational Review,* **36** (1966), 284–294.

St. John, Nancy Hoyt. *School Integration Research: The Pittsburgh Study,* unpublished monograph, April 1969.

St. John, Nancy Hoyt. "Desegregation and Minority Group Performance," *Review of Educational Research,* **40** (February 1970), 111–134.

St. John, Nancy Hoyt. "The Validity of Children's Reports of their Parents' Educational Level: ''A Methodological Note'' *Sociology of Education,* **43** (Summer 1970), 255–269.

St. John, Nancy Hoyt. "The Elementary Classroom as a Frog Pond: Self-Concept, Sense of Control and Social Context," *Social Forces,* **49** (June 1971), 581–595.

St. John, Nancy Hoyt. "Social-Psychological Aspects of School Desegregation," in Herbert Walberg, and Andrew Kopan (eds.), *Urban Education Today: Rethinking Theory and Practice,* San Francisco, Jossey-Bass, 1972(a).

St. John, Nancy Hoyt. "Desegregation: Voluntary or Mandatory?," *Integrated Education,* **10** (January/February 1972), 7–16.

St. John, Nancy Hoyt. "School Racial Context and the Aspirations of Ninth Graders," unpublished paper, 1973.

St. John, Nancy Hoyt. *"Midway to Where in Boston Schools? A Sociological Study of Sixth-Grade Children in Bi-Racial Classrooms,* unpublished monograph, March 1974.

St. John, Nancy Hoyt, and Lewis, Ralph G. "The Influence of School Racial Context on Academic Achievement," *Social Problems* **19** (Summer 1971), 68–78.

St. John, Nancy Hoyt, and Lewis, Ralph G. "Children's Interracial Friendships: An Exploration of the Contact Hypothesis," October 1973. Unpublished paper.

St. John, Nancy Hoyt, and Lewis, Ralph G. "Race and the Social Structure of the Elementary Classroom," *Sociology of Education,* in press.

Saltman, Juliet Z. *Open Housing as a Social Movement: Challenge, Conflict, and Change,* Lexington, Mass., Heath, 1971.

Samuels, Ivan G. *Desegrated Education and Differences in Academic Achievement,* unpublished doctoral dissertation, Indiana University, 1958.

Samuels, Joseph Maurice. *A Comparison of Projects Representative of Compensatory: Busing; and Non-Compensatory Programs for Inner-City Students,* unpublished doctoral dissertation, University of Connecticut, 1971.

Sanders, Lelia. *The Development of Racial Identification in Black Preschool-Age Children,* unpublished doctoral dissertation, Harvard University, 1971.

Schmuck, Richard A., and Luzki, Margaret B. "Black and White Students in Several Small Communities," *Applied Behavioral Science,* **5(2)** (1969), 203–220.

Schwartz, Michael, and Tangri, Sandra S. "A Note on Self-Concept as an Insulator Against Delinquency," *American Sociological Review,* **30** (1965), 922–926.

Scott, Lederle J. *An Analysis of the Self-Concept of Seventh Grade Students in Segregated-Desegregated Schools of Oklahoma City,* unpublished doctoral dissertation, University of Oklahoma, 1969.

Scudder, Bonnie Todd, and Jurs, Stephen G. "Do Bused Negro Children Affect Achievement of Non-Negro Children?" *Integrated Education,* **9** (March/April 1971), 30–34.

Seasholes, Bradbury. "Impact of Racial Imbalance and Balance: An Assessment by Professional Educational Research Personnel," in Board of Education, Commonwealth of Massachusetts, *Report of the Advisory Committee on Racial Imbalance and Education,* 1965, 109–118.

Sexton, Patricia C. *Education and Income, Inequalities of Opportunity in Our Public Schools,* New York, Viking Press, 1961.

Shaker Heights School Board. *An Interim Evaluation of the Shaker Schools Plan, 1970–71,* Shaker Heights, O., February 1972. (mimeographed)

Shibutani, Tamotsu. "Reference Groups and Social Control," in Arnold Rose (ed.), *Human Behavior and Social Processes,* Boston, Houghton Mifflin, 1962, 128–147.

Silberman, Charles E. *Crisis in Black and White,* New York, Random House, 1964.

Silverman, Irwin, and Shaw, Marvin E., "Effects of Sudden Mass Desegregation on Interracial Interaction and Attitudes in one Southern City," *Journal of Social Issues* **29** (No. 4) 1973, 133–142.

Simmel, Georg. *The Sociology of George Simmel,* K. Wolff (trans.), Glencoe, Ill., Free Press, 1950.

Singer, Dorothy. *Interracial Attitudes of Negro and White Fifth Grade Children in Segregated and Unsegregated Schools,* unpublished doctoral dissertation, Teachers College, Columbia University, 1966.

Slone, Irene Wholl. *The Effects of One School Pairing on Pupil Achievement, Anxieties and Attitudes,* unpublished doctoral dissertation, New York University, 1968.

Smith, M. Brewster "The Schools and Prejudice: Findings," in Charles Y. Glock and Ellen Siegelman (eds.), *Prejudice U.S.A.,* New York, Praeger, 1969.

Smith, Marshall S. "Equality of Educational Opportunity: The Basic Findings Reconsidered," in Frederick Mosteller and Daniel P. Moynihan (eds.), *On Equality of Educational Opportunity,* New York, Random House, 1972, 230–342.

Spady, William G. "The Impact of School Resources on Students," in Fred N. Kerlinger (ed.), *Review of Research in Education,* Vol. 1 in press, 1973.

Springer, Doris V. "Awareness of Racial Differences by Preschool Children in Hawaii," *Genetic Psychology Monographs,* **41** (May 1950), 215–270.

Stallings, Frank H. "A Study of the Immediate Effects of Integration on Scholastic Achievement in the Louisville Public Schools," *Journal of Negro Education,* **28** (Fall 1959), 439–444.

Stodolsky, Susan S., and Lesser, Gerald. "Learning Patterns in the Disadvantaged," *Harvard Educational Review,* **37** (Fall 1967), 546–593.

Stonequist, Everett *The Marginal Man,* New York, Scribner, 1937.

Stouffer, Samuel. A., et al. *The American Soldier,* Vol. 1, Princeton, N.J., Princeton University Press, 1949.

Strauss, Susan. "The Effect of School Integration on the Self-Concept of Negro and Puerto Rican Children," *Graduate Research in Education and Related Disciplines,* **3** (April 1967), 63–76.

Strickman, Leonard P. "Desegregation: The Metropolitan Concept," *The Urban Review,* **6** (September/October 1972), 18–23.

Suchman, Edward A., Dean, John P., and Williams, Robin M., Jr. *Desegregation: Some Propositions and Research Suggestions,* New York, Anti-Defamation League of B'Nai B'Rith, 1958.

Sullivan, Neil V. "Discussion: Implementing Equal Educational Opportunity," *Harvard Educational Review,* **38** (Winter 1968), 148–155.

Sullivan, Neil, and Stewart, Evelyn S. *Now Is the Time: Integration in the Berkeley Schools,* Bloomington, Indiana University Press, 1969.

Sutherland, Edwin H. *Principles of Criminology,* Philadelphia, Lippincott, 1955.

Taylor, Charlotte P. *Some Changes in Self-Concept in the First Year of Desegregated Schooling,* unpublished doctoral dissertation, University of Delaware, 1967.

Teele, James E., Jackson, Ellen, and Mayo, Clara. "Family Experiences in Operation Exodus: The Bussing of Negro Children," *Community Mental Health Journal,* Monograph No. 3, New York, Columbia University Press 1967.

Teele, James E., and Mayo Clara. "School Racial Integration: Tumult and Shame," *Journal of Social Issues,* **25** (1969), 137–156.

TenHouten, Warren D., et al. "School Ethnic Composition, Social Contexts, and Educational Plans of Mexican-American and Anglo High School Students," *American Journal of Sociology,* **77** (July 1971), 89–107.

Thomas, William, I. *The Unadjusted Girl,* Boston, Little, Brown, 1923.

Tumin, Melvin M. *Desegregation: Resistance and Readiness,* Princeton, N. J., Princeton University Press, 1958.

U.S. Commission on Civil Rights. *Survey of School Desegregation in the Southern and Border States, 1965–66,* Washington, D.C., U.S. Government Printing Office, February 1966.

U.S. Commission on Civil Rights. *Racial Isolation in the Public Schools,* Washington, D.C., U.S. Government Printing Office, 1967 (a).

U.S. Commission on Civil Rights. *Southern School Desegregation, 1966–67,* Washington, D.C., U.S. Government Printing Office, July 1967, (b).

U.S. Commission on Civil Rights *What Students Perceive,* Clearing House Publication No 24, Washington, D.C., 1970.

U.S. News and World Report. "Does Race Really Make a Difference in Intelligence?" (October 26, 1956), 74–75.

Useem, Elizabeth L. *White Suburban Secondary Students in Schools with Token Desegregation: Correlates of Racial Attitudes,* unpublished doctoral dissertation, Harvard University, 1971.

Van den Haag, Ernest. "Social Science Testimony in the Desegregation Cases: A Reply to Professor Kenneth Clark," *Villanova Law Review,* **6** (Fall 1960), 69–79.

Vanneman, Reeve D., and Pettigrew, Thomas F. "Race and Relative Deprivation in the Urban United States," *Race,* **13(4)** (April 1972), 461–486.

Veroff, Joseph, and Peele, Stanton. "Intial Effects of Desegregation on the Achievement Motivation of Negro Elementary School Children," *Journal of Social Issues,* **25** (3) (1969), 71–91.

Walberg, Herbert J. "An Evaluation of an Urban-Suburban School Bussing Program: Student Achievement and Perception of Class Learning Environments," Draft of Report to METCO, Cambridge, Mass., July 1, 1969.

Walker, Kenneth DeLeon. *Effects of Social and Cultural Isolation upon the Self-Concepts of Negro Children,* unpublished doctoral dissertation, University of Miami, Florida, 1968.

Wasserman, Miriam. "Busing as a 'Cover Issue'—A Radical View," *The Urban Review,* **6,** (September/October 1972), 6–10.

Webster, Staten W. "The Influence of Interracial Contact on Social Acceptance in a Newly Integrated School," *Journal of Educational Psychology,* **52** (December 1961), 292–296.

Weinberg, Meyer. *Race and Place: A Legal History of the Neighborhood School,* Washington, D.C., U.S. Department of Health, Education and Welfare, 1967.

Weinberg, Meyer. *Desegregation Research: An Appraisal,* 2nd ed. Bloomington, Ind., Phi Delta Kappa, 1970.

Weinstein, Eugene A., and Geisel, Paul N. "Family Decision Making over Desegregation," *Sociometry,* **25** (March 1962), 21–29.

Wellman, Barry. "I am a Student," *Sociology of Education,* **44** (Fall 1971), 422–437.

Wellman, Barry S. "Social Identities and Cosmopolitanism among Urban Adolescents: Variation by Race, Social Status, and School Integration Experience," unpublished doctoral dissertation, Harvard University, 1970.

Wessman, Alden E. *Evaluation of Project ABC,* Final Report of Project No. 5–0549, Washington, D.C., U.S. Department of Health, Education and Welfare, 1969.

Whitmore, Paul G., Jr. *A Study of School Desegregation: Attitude*

Change and Scale Validation, unpublished doctoral dissertation, University of Tennessee, 1956.

Williams, Daniel E. *Self-Concept and Verbal Mental Ability in Negro Pre-School Children,* unpublished doctoral dissertation, St. John's University, 1968.

Williams, Frank E. *An Analysis of Some Differences Between Negro High School Seniors from a Segregated High School and a Non-Segregated High School in Brevard County, Florida,* unpublished doctoral dissertation, University of Florida, 1968.

Williams, Robert L., and Byars, Harry. "The Effect of Academic Initegration on the Self-Esteem of Southern Negro Students," *The Journal of Social Psychology,* **80** (2) (1970), 183–188.

Williams, Robin M., Jr. *Strangers Next Door: Ethnic Relations in American Communities,* Englewood Cliffs, N.J., Prentice-Hall, 1964.

Wilson, Alan. "Educational Consequences of Segregation in a California Community," in U.S. Commission on Civil Rights, *Racial Isolation in the Public Schools,* Vol. II, Washington, D.C., 1967, 165–206.

Wilson, Alan B. *The Effect of Residential Segregation upon Educational Achievement and Aspiration,* unpublished doctoral dissertation, University of California, Berkeley, 1961.

Wilson, Robert A. "Anomie in the Ghetto: A Study of Neighborhood Type, Race and Anomie," *American Journal of Sociology,* **77** (July 1971), 66–88.

Wolf, Eleanor. "Civil Rights and Social Science Data," *Race,* **14** (October 1972), 155–182.

Wolff, Max. "Segregation in the Schools of Gary, Indiana," *Journal of Educational Sociology,* **36** (February 1963), 251–258.

Wolman, T. G. "Learning Effects of Integration in New Rochelle," *Integrated Education,* **2** (December 1964-January 1965), 30–31.

Wood, Bruce Hartley. *The Effect of Bussing vs. Non-Bussing on the Intellectual Functioning of Inner City, Disadvantaged Elementary School Children,* unpublished doctoral dissertation, University of Massachusetts, 1968.

Works, Ernest. "Residence in Integrated and Segregated Housing and

Improvement in Self-Concepts of Negroes,'' *Sociology and Social Research,* **46** (April 1962), 294–301.

Wrightstone, J. Wayne. ''Demonstration Guidance Project in New York City,'' *Harvard Educational Review,* **30** (1960), 237–251.

Wrightstone, J. Wayne, McClelland, S. D., and Forleno, G., *Evaluation of the Community Zoning Program,* New York City: Bureau of Educational Research, Board of Education, 1966.

Wylie, Ruth C. *The Self-Concept: A Critical Survey of Pertinent Literature,* Lincoln, University of Nebraska Press. 1961.

Yarrow, Leon J., and Yarrow, Marian Radke. ''Leadership and Interpersonal Change,'' *The Journal of Social Issues,* **14** (1958), 47–59.

Yarrow, Marian R., Campbell, John D., and Yarrow, Leon J. ''Acquisition of New Norms: A Study of Racial Desegregation,'' *Journal of Social Issues,* **14 (1)** (1958), 8–28.

Young, Whitney M., Jr., *To Be Equal,* New York, McGraw-Hill, 1964.

Zdep, Stanley M., and Joyce, Diane. *The Newark-Verona Plan for Sharing Educational Opportunity,* Educational Testing Service, Princeton, N.J., September 1, 1969. (mimeographed)

Zimmer, Basil G., and Hawley, Amos H. *Metropolitan Area Schools: Resistance to District Reorganization,* Beverly Hills, Calif., Sage Publication, 1968.

Zirkel, Perry A. ''Self-Concept and the 'Disadvantage' of Ethnic Group Membership and Mixture,'' *Review of Educational Research,* **41** (June 1971), 211–225.

Zirkel, Perry A., and Moses, E. Gnanaraj. ''Self-Concept and Ethnic Group Membership Among Public School Students,'' *American Educational Research Journal,* **8** (March 1971), 253–264.

Author Index

225

Subject Index

Academic achievement, effect of desegregation on, 7, 16–40, 119
measurement of, 7, 17–19
verbal versus mathematical, 30–31, 34, 37, 119
Achievement level, effect on other outcomes of desegregation, 79, 111
Afro-American studies, 125
Age, effect on outcomes of desegregation, 37, 77–78, 110, 120
American Educational Research Association, 44
Anxiety, effect of desegregation on, 46–48
influence of minority group position, 99–100
Aspiration, effect of desegregation on, 55–60, 119
Attitudes, interracial, effect of contact on, 97–99
effect of desegregation on, 7, 64–86, 119
measures of, 64–67

Behavior, interracial, effect of desegregation on, 7, 70–71, 119
factors affecting, 71–81
measures of, 64–67
Black community, 89, 91, 92, 129–130
Brown versus *Board of Education*, 42
Busing, drawbacks of, 131
effect on research design, 11
effect on black pupils, 27, 39
white pupils, 34, 35
public opinion, re, black, 130
white, 129

Case studies, of desegregated schools, 81–85
City size, effect on outcomes of desegregation, 6, 37
Community conditions, effect on outcomes of desegregation, 10, 39, 52, 76
Community control, of schools, 91–92, 130
Comparison group, choice of, 12, 13
Compensatory programs, 11, 26, 39
Constitutional mandate, for desegregation, 118, 136

Index of Cities
and States